Table of Con

How to Use This Book

- Choose the bulletin board you want to create.
- Read the directions and gather materials.
- Adjust the design of the board to fit the size of your bulletin board.
- Laminate the full-color caption letters and additional color cutouts. You will find complete directions for using these on page 68. Letters and color cutouts begin on page 69.
- Follow the directions to complete the board.
- Add your own original touches and student work.

Good Work Machine

Materials

- background—yellow butcher paper
- machine:
  large box top
  blue butcher paper or Con-Tact® paper
- black construction paper scrap (for plug)
- black yarn
- blank paper—two sheets
- assorted construction paper for mounting student work
- cutouts:
  caption on pages 69 and 71, laminated and trimmed
  "beep" signs on page 73, laminated and trimmed
  machine face on page 75, laminated and trimmed
  on, off, in, and out signs on page 77, laminated and trimmed

Put It Together

1. Cover the bulletin board with yellow butcher paper.

2. Cover the box top with blue paper. Make slits with scissors.

3. Tape a page of student's work in the "in" slot. Randomly pin other students' finished work coming out of the "out" slot and scattered across the board.

4. Attach the face and sign cutouts (pages 75 and 77) to the box. Then add the black yarn and plug to complete the machine.

5. Pin the box to the bulletin board.

6. Pin the caption to the board. Scatter "beep" signs (page 73) around the board.

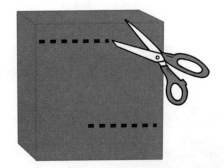

Other Ways to Use This Board

Use the bulletin board to challenge students to use creative thinking. Write a problem to be solved on a sheet of paper to go "in" at the top of the board. Students write a solution to the problem. Post these coming "out" of the machine.

For example:

   Problem—lost house key and no one is home

   Problem—a fight with your best friend

   Problem—missed the bus after school

Ropin' in Mighty Fine Work

Materials

- background:
  sky—blue butcher paper
  ground—yellow butcher paper

- cowboy:
  shirt and arms—two 12" x 18" (30.5 x 45.5 cm) red construction paper
  jeans—12" x 18" (30.5 x 45.5 cm) dark blue construction paper
  hat and gloves—12" x 18" (30.5 x 45.5 cm) brown construction paper
  rope—jump rope or roving
  neckerchief—blue cotton handkerchief

- red construction paper for mounting student work

- cutouts:
  caption on pages 79, 81, and 83, laminated and trimmed
  cowboy's head on page 85, laminated and trimmed
  cowboy's boots on pages 87 and 89, laminated and trimmed

Put It Together

1. Cover the bulletin board with blue butcher paper. Add a strip of yellow butcher paper "ground" along the bottom of the board.

2. Cut clothing from construction paper as shown. Add details with a black marking pen.

3. Pin the body pieces together on the bulletin board, along with the head and boots (pages 85, 87, and 89). Pin the neckerchief below the cowboy's head. Bend one arm to hold the rope.

4. Pin the rope to the board, forming a large loop.

5. Pin the caption to the bottom of the board. Add student work.

shirt front

arms

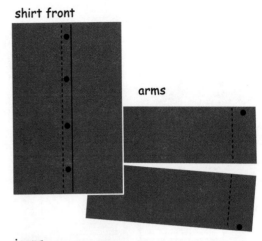

jeans

hat and gloves

boots-pages 87 and 89

head-page 85

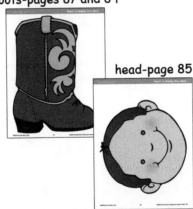

Other Ways to Use This Board

Cover "Work" with a sign saying "Words." Write words related to being a cowhand on strips of tagboard, for example:

cowboy, cowgirl, cowpoke, lasso, range, wrangler, chuck wagon, doggie

Students find the meaning of the words and use them in sentences or stories.

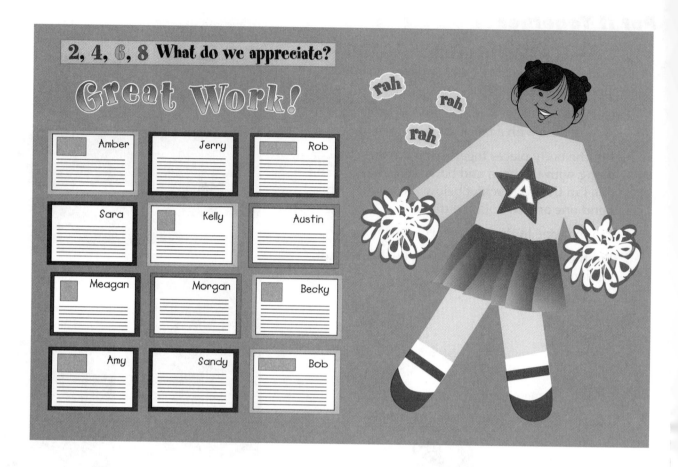

Rah! Rah! Great Work!

Materials

- background—blue butcher paper
- cheerleader:
  sweater and arms—12" x 18" (30.5 x 45.5 cm) yellow construction paper
  legs—9" x 12" (23 x 30.5 cm) flesh-colored construction paper
  shoes—9" x 12" (23 x 30.5 cm) red construction paper
  socks—two 5 1/2" x 8 1/2" (14 x 21 cm) pieces of white paper
  skirt—red crepe paper or tissue paper
- pompoms—blue and white tissue paper; string
- assorted construction paper for mounting student work
- cutouts:
  caption on page 91, laminated and trimmed
  sentence strips on page 93, laminated and trimmed
  cheerleader's face on page 95, laminated and trimmed
  star for sweater on page 97, laminated and trimmed
  "rah" signs on page 97, laminated and trimmed

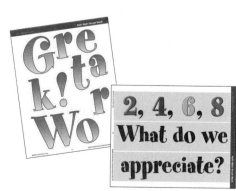

Put It Together

1. Cover the bulletin board with blue butcher paper.

2. Lightly sketch the body parts on construction paper as shown. Cut out all the parts.

3. To make the shoes, fold the red construction paper in half and cut two straps and two shoe tops. Glue them to the white paper, then trim the edges so that they are the width of the cheerleader's legs. Glue these to the legs.

4. Pleat the tissue paper or crepe paper to make the cheerleader's skirt.

5. Pin the body parts together on the bulletin board. Glue the star (page 97) to the sweater. Pin the top of the skirt only. Spread the pleats apart to give a 3-D look to the skirt.

6. Cut blue and white tissue paper into strips for the pompoms. Tie the strips together with string. Pin the pompoms to the ends of the sleeves.

7. Pin the caption and sentence strips to the bulletin board. Pin the "rah" signs around the cheerleader.

8. Add student work.

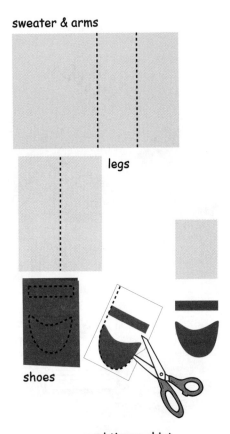

sweater & arms

legs

shoes

red tissue skirt

blue and white tissue pompoms

Other Ways to Use This Board

Have students write cheers for the class, school, teacher, principal, etc. Post these on the bulletin board.

2, 4, 6, 8
Who do we appreciate?
Mrs. Brown
Rah! Rah! Rah!

Working together
Is just fine
We're the kids
From Room 29

What Delicious Work

Materials

- background—yellow and blue butcher paper
- crocodile:
  body—green butcher paper, wrapping paper, or plastic tablecloth
- assorted construction paper for mounting student work
- cutouts:
  caption on pages 99 and 101, laminated and trimmed
  eyes on page 103, laminated and trimmed
  bird on page 105, laminated and trimmed
  fish on page 107, laminated and trimmed

Put It Together

1. Cover the top half of the bulletin board with yellow butcher paper.

2. Cut a crocodile from green butcher paper to fit the bulletin board. Pin the crocodile in place.

3. Cut a strip of blue butcher paper with a "wavy" top to represent water. Pin this across the bottom of the board.

4. Cut out the eyes (page 103) and the bird (page 105) and pin them on to the crocodile. Add a big smile with a black marking pen.

5. Pin the caption to the bulletin board.

6. Add student work. Pin the fish (page 107) among student work papers.

yellow butcher paper

crocodile

"wavy" water

Other Ways to Use This Board

Each student finds an interesting fact about crocodiles and writes it on a sentence strip. Post these facts on the crocodile's back.

A crocodile is a reptile.   Crocodiles have scales.

Then students use the information to write crocodile reports.

Something to Spout About!

Materials

- background:
  water—blue butcher paper
  sky—yellow butcher paper

- whale:
  body—black butcher paper
  tail—smaller piece of black butcher paper
  eye—scrap of white construction paper
  spout—white tissue paper

- assorted construction paper for mounting student work

- cutouts—caption on pages 109, 111, and 113,
  laminated and trimmed

Put It Together

1. Cover the top half of the bulletin board with yellow butcher paper.

2. Measure out blue butcher paper to fill the rest of the board. Cut waves across the top and pin the paper in place.

3. Lay black butcher paper on the floor for the whale's body. Round the top corners as shown. Slip this sheet behind the blue paper and staple in place.

4. Fold the remaining black paper in half. Cut on the fold as shown to make the whale's tail. Open and pin it in place on the bulletin board.

5. Round the corners of a white rectangle for the eye. Add the eyeball with a black marking pen. Pin it in place on the whale.

6. Crumple white tissue paper to form the spout. Pin it in place.

7. Pin the caption to the bulletin board.

8. Add student work.

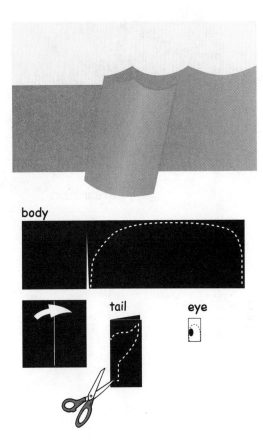

body

tail

eye

Other Ways to Use This Board

- display student stories or reports about whales
- display fiction and/or nonfiction books about whales
- list whale facts on sentence strips
- display student drawings of different types of whales

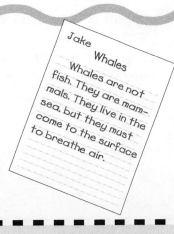

Jake

Whales

Whales are not fish. They are mammals. They live in the sea, but they must come to the surface to breathe air.

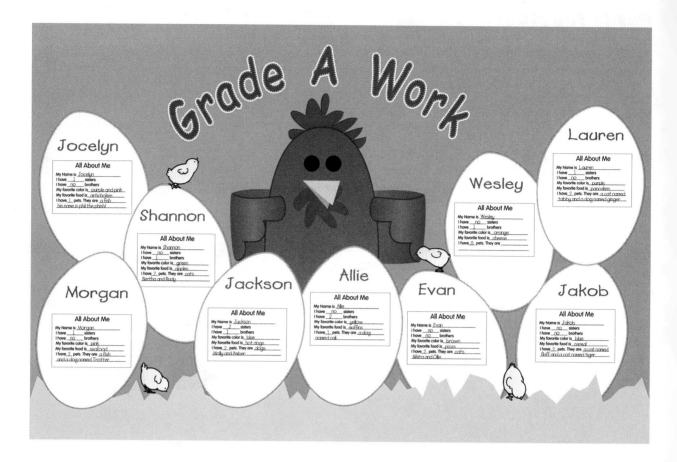

Grade A Work

Materials

- background—blue and yellow butcher paper
- hen:
  body and wings—two 12" x 18" (30.5 x 45.5 cm) brown construction paper
  comb and wattle—scraps of red construction paper
  beak—scrap of yellow construction paper
  eyes—two black buttons
- eggs—a supply of 12" x 18" (30.5 x 45.5 cm) white construction paper
- cutouts:
  caption on page 115 and 117, laminated and trimmed
  chicks on page 119, laminated and trimmed

Put It Together

1. Cover the bulletin board with blue butcher paper. Cut a zigzag line of yellow butcher paper. Pin it along the bottom of the board.

2. Cut one egg per student from white construction paper. Write their names with marking pen. Pin the eggs around the bulletin board.

3. Lightly sketch the parts of the hen as shown. Cut out the parts and glue them together. Roll the wings slightly to give dimension to the hen. Glue only the bottom half of the beak, and fold the top down to give a 3-D look. Glue on black buttons for eyes. Pin the hen to the bulletin board.

4. Cut out the chicks (page 119). Pin the chicks and the caption to the board.

5. Pin up student work on each student's "personalized" egg.

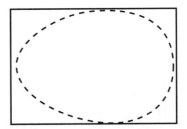

hen body   wings

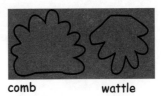

comb   wattle

beak

Other Ways to Use This Board

Use the eggs for a matching center. Write words on cards. Pin the cards to the eggs on the bulletin board. Students find matches and write them on a sheet of paper.

Words to use:

- contractions
- abbreviations
- compound words

"You can!" said Toucan

Materials

- background—blue butcher paper or fabric
- toucan:
  head—6" (15 cm) square of black construction paper
         4" (10 cm) square of yellow construction paper
  wings and tail—12" x 18" (30.5 x 45.5 cm) black construction paper
  eye—"wiggle" eye or black marking pen
  body—12" x 18" (30.5 x 45.5 cm) red construction paper
  beak and feet—9" x 12" (23 x 30.5 cm) orange construction paper
- perch—scraps of brown construction paper
- assorted construction paper for mounting student work
- cutouts—caption on pages 121 and 123, laminated and trimmed

Put It Together

1. Cover the bulletin board with blue butcher paper or fabric.

2. Cut the toucan from construction paper as shown. Glue the parts together.

3. Glue a "wiggle" eye in the yellow head circle (or add an eye with a black marking pen).

4. Cut a perch from brown paper scraps. Pin it to the bulletin board. Pin the toucan on the board so it appears to be standing on the perch.

5. Pin the caption to the bulletin board.

6. Mount student work on colorful construction paper and pin it to the board.

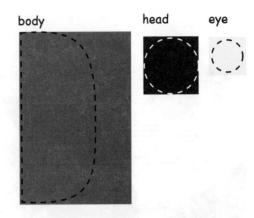

body   head   eye

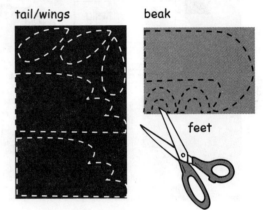

tail/wings   beak

feet

Other Ways to Use This Board

Students write acrostics to post on the bulletin board. (Provide the topic—birds, rainforest animals, colors.) Post a sample on the board as an example.

Tropical bird

Over-sized bill

Unique

Colorful

Ate fruit with a

Narrow tongue

A Flock of Good Work

Materials

- background:
  sky—blue butcher paper
  hill—green butcher paper

- for each lamb:
  body—12" x 18" (30.5 x 45.5 cm) white construction paper
  topknot—cotton batting
  legs, head, and ear—12" x 18" (30.5 x 45.5 cm) black construction paper
  nose—pink paper scrap
  eye—"wiggle" eye

- cutouts:
  caption on pages 125 and 127, laminated and trimmed
  "baa" signs on page 129, laminated and trimmed

Put It Together

1. Cover the top half of the bulletin board with blue butcher paper. Cut a tall hill from green butcher paper. Pin it to the bulletin board.

2. Cut each lamb's body from white construction paper. Pin the bodies to the bulletin board.

3. Cut out the head, ears, and legs from black paper as shown.

4. Glue the parts of the head together. Glue on the pink nose and "wiggle" eye. Add a topknot cut from cotton batting to each head. Pin the parts to the bulletin board.

5. Pin the legs to the board.

6. Pin the caption and "baa" cards to the board.

7. Pin student work on the lambs.

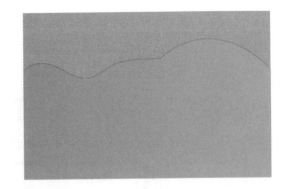

body

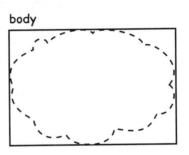

head   ear   legs

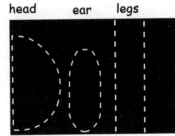

Other Ways to Use This Board

Replace the word "Work" in the caption with "Words." Use the board to display:

- spelling words
- words describing sheep
- phrases using collectives (a flock of sheep, a herd of cattle, a school of fish, etc.)

Students use the words as they write sentences, paragraphs, or stories.

No Monkey Business Here

Materials

- background—green butcher paper
- monkey:
  head and ears—12" x 18" (30.5 x 45.5 cm) brown construction paper
  face and inside ears—9" x 12" (23 x 30.5 cm) pink construction paper
  arms—12" x 18" (30.5 x 45.5 cm) brown construction paper
  hands—9" x 12" (23 x 30.5 cm) brown construction paper
- purple construction paper for mounting student work
- cutouts:
  caption on pages 131 and 133, laminated and trimmed
  bananas on page 135, laminated and trimmed

Put It Together

1. Cover the bulletin board with green butcher paper.

2. Cut out the monkey parts as shown. Create hands by tracing around your own hands.

3. Cut the face and inner ears from pink paper. Glue the monkey's face to the head. Add facial features with a black marking pen. Glue the inner ears to the outer ears. Glue the ears to the head.

4. Pin the monkey's head to the upper center of the bulletin board. Pin the arms across the board, using two brown pieces for each arm. Pin the hands to the ends of the arms. Pin a banana in each hand.

5. Pin the caption to the board. Add student work.

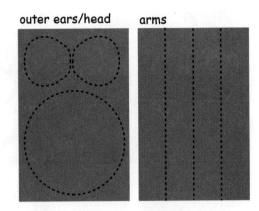
outer ears/head   arms

hands

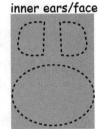
inner ears/face

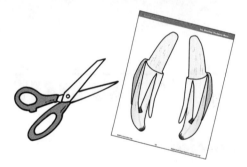

Other Ways to Use This Board

Write common expressions on sentence strips and post them on the bulletin board. Discuss their meanings with students. Then have students select one or more to use in writing sentences or short stories.

slow as the seven year itch

quiet as a mouse

in the blink of an eye

quick as a wink

stick out your neck

a green thumb

get up on the wrong side of the bed

time to hit the hay

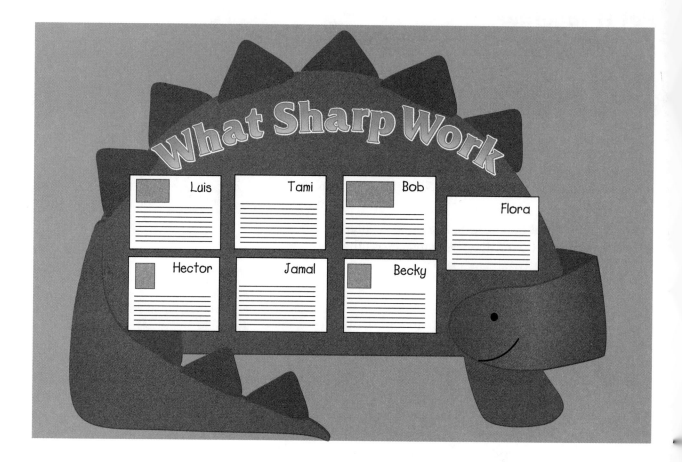

What Sharp Work

Materials

- background—blue butcher paper
- dinosaur—orange butcher paper
- cutouts—caption on pages 137 and 139, laminated and trimmed

Put It Together

1. Cover the bulletin board with blue butcher paper.

2. Cut out a large hill-shaped piece of orange butcher paper for the dinosaur's body. Pin it to the bulletin board.

3. Cut a head, tail, front foot, and spikes from orange paper. Add facial details with a marking pen. Pin all of the pieces to the bulletin board. Curl the end of the tail and the head forward for a 3-D look.

4. Add the caption. Pin student work on the dinosaur's body.

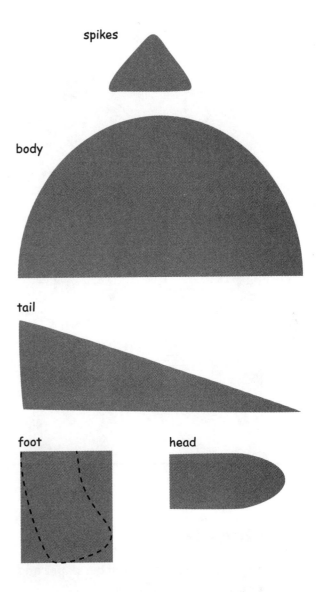

spikes

body

tail

foot   head

Other Ways to Use This Board

Select several dinosaur books. Write one or more questions that can be answered by reading the book. Post the question(s) and the book's cover (or name) on the dinosaur's body. Students select a question and book, read to find the answer, and write it on lined paper.

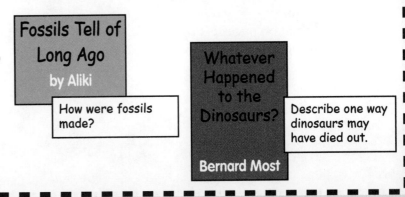

Fossils Tell of Long Ago
by Aliki

How were fossils made?

Whatever Happened to the Dinosaurs?

Bernard Most

Describe one way dinosaurs may have died out.

What Purr-fect Work

Materials

- background—blue butcher paper and colorful fabric
- cat:
  body—12" x 18" (30.5 x 45.5 cm) orange construction paper
  head, ears, paws, tail—12" x 18" (30.5 x 45.5 cm) orange construction paper
  nose—scrap of pink construction paper
  whiskers—pieces of black pipe cleaner
- assorted construction paper for mounting student work
- cutouts:
  caption on pages 141 and 143, laminated and trimmed
  toy mouse on page 145, laminated and trimmed

Put It Together

1. Cover the bulletin board with blue butcher paper. Add a strip of colorful fabric across the bottom half of the board.

2. Lightly sketch the cat's parts as shown on orange construction paper. Cut out the pieces.

3. Cut a nose from a pink paper scrap. Glue it to the face. Add other details to the face with a black marking pen. Glue on pipe cleaner whiskers and the ears.

4. Pin the cat's body to the bulletin board. Pin the mouse (page 145) in the cat's paws.

5. Add the caption. Pin student work on the fabric.

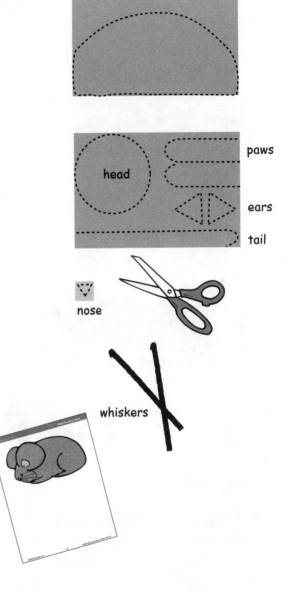

Other Ways to Use This Board

Use this purr-fect bulletin board to introduce onomatopoeia (a word that imitates a sound). Post several "sound" words on the board. Provide blank cards for students to use in writing other sound words to go on the board.

Hip Hippo-Ray!

Materials

- background—red and yellow butcher paper
- hippo:
  body, head, ears, legs—blue butcher paper
  nostrils—two small paper cups
  toenails—six bottle caps
  eyes—two large black buttons
  tail—piece of gray or pink roving
- plastic flower
- cutouts—caption on pages 147 and 149, laminated and trimmed

Put It Together

1. Cover the bulletin board with yellow butcher paper. Add a red strip across the bottom.

2. Cut the hippo's body parts from blue butcher paper as shown. Make them as large as possible. Pin the pieces to the bulletin board.

3. Pin the paper cups on the face for nostrils.

4. Glue on button eyes or draw eyes with a black marking pen.

5. Glue on the bottle caps for toenails.

6. Add a strip of roving for the tail and pin a plastic flower in the hippo's mouth.

7. Pin the caption to the bulletin board. Pin student work on the hippo's body.

body

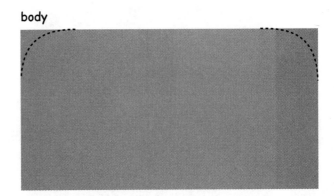

head

legs

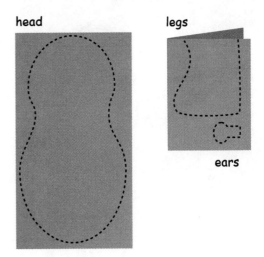

ears

Other Ways to Use This Board

Ask students to write about a big accomplishment from their own lives—something that deserves a "Hippo-ray!" Post these on the bulletin board.

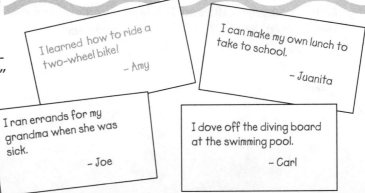

I learned how to ride a two-wheel bike!
– Amy

I can make my own lunch to take to school.
– Juanita

I ran errands for my grandma when she was sick.
– Joe

I dove off the diving board at the swimming pool.
– Carl

We All Pull Together

Materials

- background—green butcher paper
- caterpillar:
  body—assorted 12" (30.5 cm) construction circles in bright colors
  antennae—black pipe cleaners
- flower—green construction scraps for leaves and stems
- cutouts:
  caption on pages 151 and 153, laminated and trimmed
  flower on page 155, laminated and trimmed

Put It Together

1. Cover the bulletin board with green butcher paper.

2. Cut one colored circle for each student in your class, plus one for the caterpillar's head. You may want to have each student design his or her segment using stripes, polka dots, or plaids.

3. Using marking pens, add details to the caterpillar's head. Cut small slits in the head. Lap the paper over and glue together to give a 3-D look to the head. Tape the pipe cleaner antennae to the back of the head.

4. Pin the caterpillar to the bulletin board.

5. Cut out the flower (page 155) and pin it to the board. Cut a stem and leaves from green construction paper for the flower. Cut a second stem and leaf to pin in the caterpillar's mouth.

6. Pin the caption to the bulletin board. Add student work.

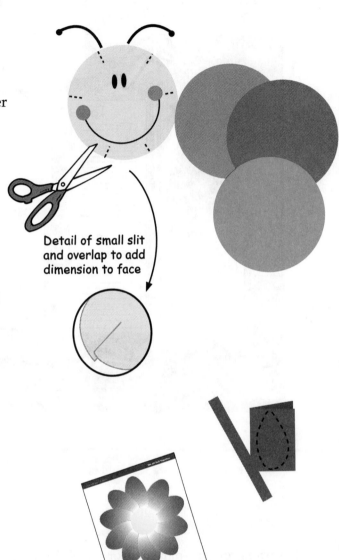

Detail of small slit and overlap to add dimension to face

Other Ways to Use This Board

Use the same caterpillar to display other material.

- class pictures and autobiographies, one segment for each student
- scientific facts about caterpillars/butterflies, one per segment
- one math problem per segment
- a story prompt on each segment

All Caught Up in Good Work

Materials

- background—dark blue or purple butcher paper
- for each spider:
  body—one small red paper plate
  legs—eight black pipe cleaners
  eyes—two black beads
- web—white poster paint and brush
- white yarn or string
- assorted construction paper for mounting student work
- cutouts—caption on pages 157, 159, and 161, laminated and trimmed

Put It Together

1. Cover the bulletin board with dark blue or purple butcher paper.

2. Pin the caption at the top of the board.

3. Using white paint, create a spider web filling the whole bulletin board. (Begin in the center and work your way to the outside edges.) Leave the area around the caption clear.

4. Make the spiders from paper plates.

   Glue beads on for eyes. Add a smile with a black marking pen.

   Tape on eight pipe cleaners to create legs. Bend the pipe cleaners to form knees and feet.

   Punch a hole in the top of each spider. Tie on a strip of white yarn. Hang the spiders from the top of the bulletin board, dangling down over the web.

5. Pin student work on the spider web.

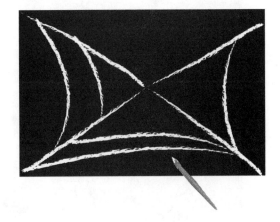

Other Ways to Use This Board

Have students write nonfiction paragraphs about spiders. Display their paragraphs on the web.

Carlos

Spiders

Spiders have eight legs. Some spiders spin webs to catch insects. The spiders eat the insects.

Anna

Trapdoor Spider

A trapdoor spider makes a burrow. It lines the burrow with silk. It covers the opening with a door. When an insect walks by, the spider pops out and catches it.

Dog-gone Good Work

Materials

- background—blue butcher paper
- doghouse—orange butcher paper with black butcher paper door
- dogs—12" (30.5 cm) squares of white, light brown, and gray construction paper
- sun—12" x 18" (30.5 x 45.5 cm) yellow construction paper
- bones—white, manila, or yellow construction paper (use pattern)
- cutouts:
  caption on pages 163 and 165, laminated and trimmed
  bone pattern on page 165
  "woof" signs on page 167, laminated and trimmed

Put It Together

1. Cover the bulletin board with blue butcher paper. Cut a large orange doghouse as shown. Use black butcher paper to cut the doghouse door.

2. Cut a sun from yellow construction paper. Pin the sun peeking out from behind the doghouse.

3. Make several folded paper dogs following the steps shown. Add details with marking or jelly pens. Pin the dogs to the bulletin board. Add the "woof" signs near two of the dogs.

4. Make a bone for each student. Write a name on each bone and then pin them to the bulletin board above student work.

5. Pin the caption to the board.

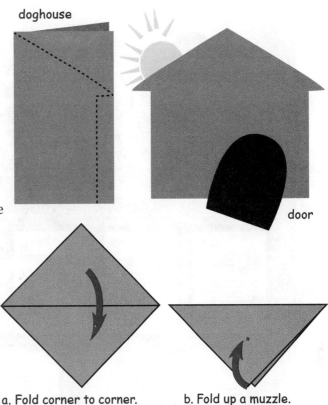

a. Fold corner to corner.   b. Fold up a muzzle.

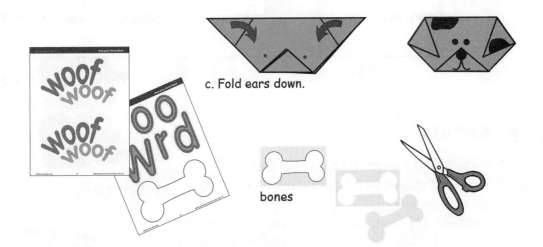

c. Fold ears down.

bones

Other Ways to Use This Board

Make a class helper's chart using as many dogs as you have class jobs. Cut a collar for each dog from construction paper scraps. Write the job on the dog's collar. Make a bone (see pattern on page 165) for each student. Pin the bone by the dog to show who is to do that job. Change the bones each week.

Joseph — Line Leader   Ambria — Calendar   Fernando — Roll Call

These Little Mice...

Materials

- background—bright blue butcher paper
  (or wrapping paper with a small pattern)

- for each mouse:
  head—9" (23 cm) square of gray construction paper
  ear—5" (13 cm) square of gray construction paper
  eyes—two black beans
  nose—small pink pompon

- assorted construction paper for mounting student work

- cutouts—caption on pages 169, 171, 173, and 175,
  laminated and trimmed

Put It Together

1. Cover the bulletin board with bright blue butcher paper or patterned wrapping paper.

2. Make mice from gray construction paper. (The number will depend on the size of your bulletin board.) There is only one ear per mouse because they are pinned together as a border. (You will need two ears for the first mouse in the row.)

3. Attach black bean eyes with white glue.

4. Attach pink pompon nose with white glue.

5. After the mice dry, pin them in a row across the top of the bulletin board.

6. Pin the caption under the row of mice. Add student work.

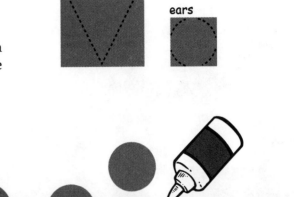

head

ears

Other Ways to Use This Board

Use the bulletin board to make a center for word family practice.

Make a chart as an example. Write word endings on tagboard strips. Students choose an ending, and then create a list of words in that word family.

| _____ice | _____est | _____ight | _____own |
| _____ust | _____un | _____ink | _____ought |

Lara

mice
nice
rice
twice
price

Aaron

fun
bun
run
sun

This Work Is Out of This World!

Materials

- background—dark blue or black butcher paper
- astronaut—all pieces from white or shiny metallic silver tagboard:
  body—12" x 18" (30.5 x 45.5 cm)
  head—12" x 12" (30.5 x 30.5 cm) square
  arms—12" x 18" (30.5 x 45.5 cm)
  mitts—two 6" x 6" (15 x 15 cm) squares
  air hose—9" x 6" (23 x 15 cm)
- stars—yellow construction paper (use pattern)
- red construction paper for mounting student work and detail stripes on astronaut
- cutouts:
  caption on pages 177, 179, and 181, laminated and trimmed
  "Wow" sign on page 183, laminated and trimmed
  face mask on page 185, laminated and trimmed
  flag on page 185, laminated and trimmed
  star pattern on page 185

Put It Together

1. Cover the bulletin board in dark blue or black butcher paper.

2. Cut out the parts of the astronaut from white or shiny metallic silver tagboard. Add strips of red construction paper as detail.

3. Glue the face mask (page 185) to the head circle. Glue the flag cutout (page 185) to the body.

4. Pin the body parts together on the bulletin board.

5. Using the pattern (page 185), cut a yellow star for each student and label it with his or her name.

6. Add the caption, sign, and student work to the board. Pin a star by each student's work.

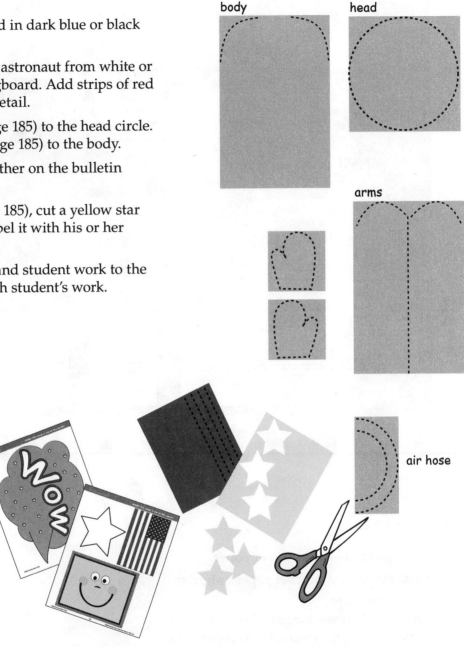

body

head

arms

air hose

Other Ways to Use This Board

Remove "This work is" leaving the caption "out of this world."

Post cards containing space words. Students use the dictionary to find the meaning of each word and use it in a sentence.

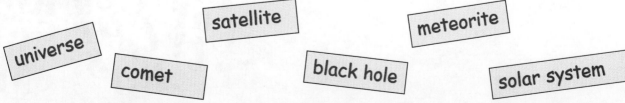

satellite

meteorite

universe

comet

black hole

solar system

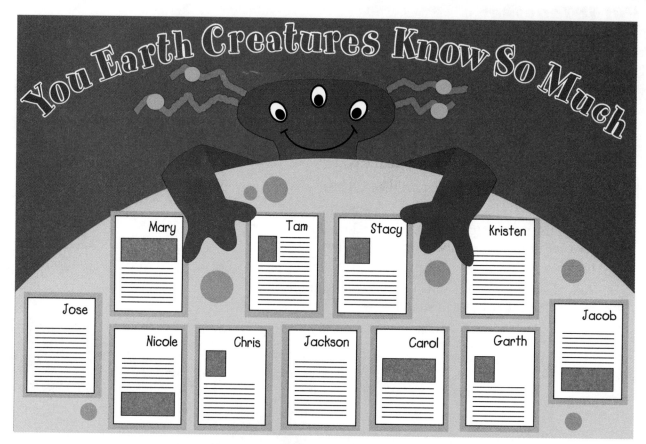

You Earth Creatures Know So Much

Materials

- background—blue butcher paper
- planet—yellow butcher paper or burlap
- space creature:
  head and arms—magenta butcher paper
  antennae—pipe cleaners and paper scraps
- cutouts:
  caption on pages 187, 189, and 191, laminated and trimmed
  eyes and craters on page 193, laminated and trimmed

Put It Together

1. Cover the top half of the bulletin board with blue butcher paper.

2. Roll out yellow butcher paper and cut a "hill" to fit the lower half of the board. Glue the craters on the planet.

3. Sketch the body parts lightly on the magenta paper. Make them as large as possible. Cut out the parts.

4. Glue three eyes to the creature's face. Add other details with a black marking pen.

5. Cut out small paper circles and push them onto the ends of the pipe cleaners. Bend or curl the pipe cleaners and tape them to the back of the head. Pin the creature's head to the bulletin board.

6. Pin the arms in place, bending them over the top of the yellow paper.

7. Pin the caption across the top of the board. Add student work.

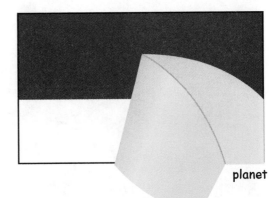

planet

head

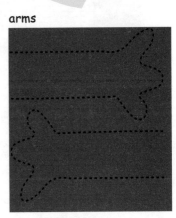

arms

pipe cleaners

Other Ways to Use This Board

Post word cards containing homographs. Students are to select a word and write a sentence using each of its meanings. Select sentences from student work to post with each word card.

> ### well
> The farmer dug a well in his field.
> The doctor gave me medicine to help me get well.

well, yard, rest, stick, mean, ball, fan, blow, bark, present

This Work Does Compute!

Materials

- background—any bright color of butcher paper
- robot:
  head—dinner-size paper plate
  eyes—two large buttons
  nose—pink eraser
  mouth—ice-cream stick
  antennas—two pencils
  ears—silver cupcake liners
  body—shoebox
  arms and legs—four paper towel rolls
  feet—two juice cans
  hands—six clothespins
- aluminum foil
- cutouts:
  caption on pages 195 and 197, laminated and trimmed
  heart and instrument panel on page 199, laminated and trimmed

Put It Together

1. Cover the bulletin board with brightly-colored butcher paper.

2. Create the robot's parts by covering the paper plate, paper towel rolls, shoebox, and juice cans with aluminum foil.

3. Assemble the head.

   Glue on the buttons, eraser, and ice-cream stick to form the face. Push the pencils into the top of the plate for the antennas.

4. Glue the heart and instrument panel (page 199) on the shoebox to make the body.

5. Pin the head and body to the bulletin board. Pin the cupcake liners next to the paper plate for ears.

6. Pin the arms and legs in place on the board. Add the juice cans for feet. Clip three clothespins to the end of each arm for hands.

7. Pin the caption to the board. Add student work.

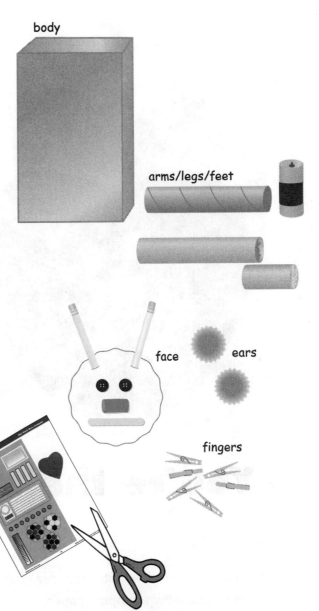

body

arms/legs/feet

face   ears

fingers

Other Ways to Use This Board

The *r* in *robot* is great for alliteration. Have students create alliterative phrases or sentences about a robot. Post these on the bulletin board.

rusty robots rattle

a robot ran rapidly

Ricky the robot ran 'round and 'round

You're the apple of my eye!

Materials

- background—yellow butcher paper
- apple—red shiny wrapping paper
- leaves—12" x18" (30.5 x 45.5 cm) green construction paper
- stem—6" x18"(15 x 45.5 cm) green construction paper
- assorted construction paper for mounting student work
- cutouts:
  caption on pages 201 and 203, laminated and trimmed
  worm on page 205, laminated and trimmed

Put It Together

1. Cover the bulletin board with yellow butcher paper.

2. Cut the apple from shiny red paper. Make it as large as possible.

3. Pin it to the board. Print students' names on the apple with a black permanent marker.

4. Cut the stem and leaves from green construction paper. Fold the leaves down the middle. Pin only one end to give the leaves a 3-D look.

5. Cut out the worm (page 205). Pin it onto the apple as shown.

6. Pin the caption to the bulletin board. Add student work.

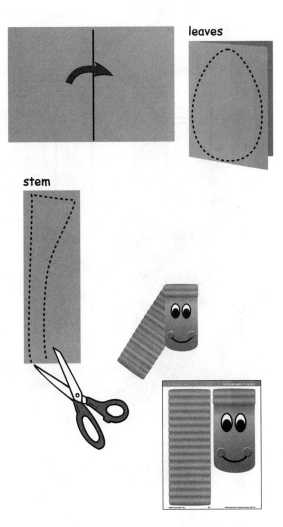

leaves

stem

Other Ways to Use This Board

Use the apple board to post class helpers. Make an apple for each class job. Make an apple leaf for each student. Pin the apples to the board. Add a leaf to each apple to show who is to do the job. Change the leaves once a week.

You are a HUGE success!

Materials

- background—blue butcher paper or fabric
- elephant:
  cheeks—pink construction paper scraps
  head, trunk, and ears—newspaper
- assorted construction paper for mounting student work
- cutouts:
  caption on pages 207, 209, and 211, laminated and trimmed
  "peanut" signs on pages 213 and 215, laminated and trimmed
  eyes on page 211, laminated and trimmed

Put It Together

1. Cover the bulletin board with blue paper or fabric.

2. Make the elephant as large as possible from newspaper. Begin with three sheets of newspaper arranged as shown. Pin the paper to the bulletin board.

3. Accordion fold a fourth sheet of newspaper for the elephant's trunk. Pin the trunk to the elephant's head. Tape or pin the peanuts (pages 213 and 215) to the end of the elephant's trunk.

4. Pin the eyes (page 211) to the head. Cut cheeks from pink construction paper and glue them to the elephant's face.

5. Pin the caption to the bulletin board. Pin student work on the elephant's ears.

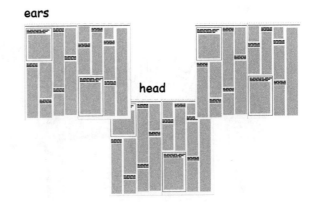

ears

head

accordion fold the trunk

cheeks

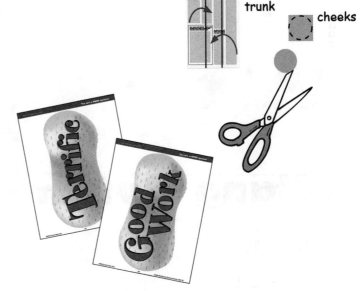

Other Ways to Use This Board

Remove the caption and add a sign saying "About Elephants." Have students write descriptions of elephants to post on the bulletin board. The descriptions may be in the form of a paragraph, list, or poem.

Megan

Elephants

Elephants are big! They have b[ ]
ears and big feet. They have a
long nose called a trunk.

Elephants eat most of the day.
They drink a lot of water too.

An Elephant Family

The father is a bull.
The mother is a cow.
The baby is a calf.
George

Hang Out the Good News!

Materials

- background:
  sky—blue butcher paper
  sun—yellow butcher paper, yellow tempera paint
- clothesline—heavy twine
- small clothespins
- large pushpins
- spray glitter
- assorted construction paper for mounting student work
- cutouts—caption on pages 217, 219, and 221, laminated and trimmed

Put It Together

1. Cover the bulletin board with blue butcher paper.

2. Cut yellow butcher paper to form a "hill" shape to place at the bottom of the board. Paint yellow rays coming from the sun. Spray glitter paint on the sun for extra sparkle.

3. Stretch the twine between two pushpins to create a clothesline. Allow as much slack as fits your board. Staple both ends of the line for greater security.

4. Pin the caption to the bulletin board. Use small clothespins to hang student work along the line.

Other Ways to Use This Board

Use the bulletin board to display articles from newspapers and magazines that students bring to share with the class.

"The time has come..."

Materials

- background:
  sky—yellow butcher paper
  water—blue butcher paper

- walrus:
  head—brown butcher paper or brown textured fabric
  snout—9" x 12" (23 x 30.5 cm) black construction paper
  whiskers—toothpicks
  tusks—9" x 12" (23 x 30.5 cm) yellow construction paper

- assorted construction paper for mounting student work

- cutouts—caption strips on pages 223, 225, 227, and 229, laminated and trimmed

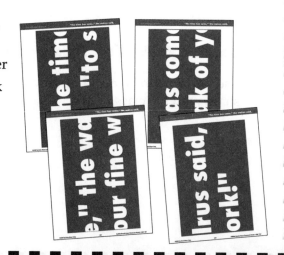

Put It Together

1. Cover the top third of the bulletin board with yellow butcher paper. Cover the rest of the board with blue butcher paper that has been cut to resemble waves.

2. Cut a large piece of brown butcher paper or fabric in the shape of a hill for the walrus's head.

3. Cut out the walrus's snout from black paper. Glue on toothpicks for bristly whiskers.

4. Cut tusks from yellow construction paper.

5. Glue the snout and tusks to the walrus's head. Add eyes with a black marking pen.

6. Pin the walrus to the bulletin board. Let the tusks hang into the blue section.

7. Pin the caption strips to the board. Add student work.

head

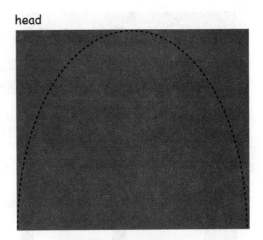

snout

tusks

whiskers

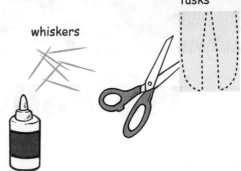

Other Ways to Use This Board

Cover "your fine work" with a sentence strip saying "many things!" Use the board to display sentence strips showing students' correct use of quotation marks. Have each student complete a sentence strip. Pin the strips in the blue part of the bulletin board.

Tara said, "This lava rock is light."

"You will like this book," said John.

We deliver the best!

Materials

- background—blue butcher paper
- truck:
  trailer—red butcher paper
  cab—orange butcher paper
  tires—black butcher paper
  hubcaps—yellow construction paper
- road—black roving
- cutouts:
  sign on page 231, laminated and trimmed
  caption on pages 233 and 235, laminated and trimmed
  truck driver on page 237, laminated and trimmed
  stars on page 239, laminated and trimmed

Put It Together

1. Cover the bulletin board with blue paper.

2. Cut a piece of red butcher paper for the trailer of the truck.

3. Use a strip of orange butcher paper for the truck cab that is half as long as the length of the trailer. Cut a square out of the corner as shown.

4. Pin the trailer and cab to the bulletin board.

5. Cut three tires from the black butcher paper and three hubcaps from yellow construction paper. Pin them in place on the bulletin board.

6. Pin black roving as a road line under the tires.

7. Pin the truck driver (page 237) to the cab. Pin the sign "Star Truckers" (page 231) to the side of the cab. Glue stars (page 239) to the cab.

8. Add the caption and student work to the board.

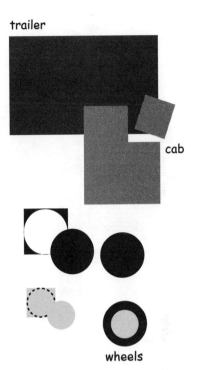

trailer

cab

wheels

Other Ways to Use This Board

Have students use the 5 W's to write a paragraph about the truck. They are to answer these questions in their paragraphs:

- Who is driving the truck?
- What is being hauled?
- Where is it going?
- When will it be delivered?
- Why is it being transported?

Post the completed paragraphs on the bulletin board.

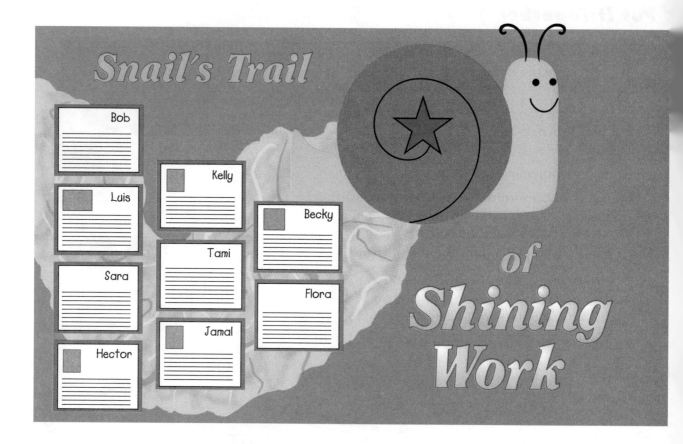

Snail's Trail of Shining Work

Materials

- background—green butcher paper
- snail:
  shell—light brown tagboard
  head and tail—two 12" x 18" (30.5 x 45.5 cm) yellow construction paper
  tentacles—pieces of black pipe cleaner
- trail—clear plastic wrap
- construction paper for mounting student work
- cutouts:
  caption on pages 241, 243, 245, and 247, laminated and trimmed
  star on page 247, laminated and trimmed

Put It Together

1. Cover the bulletin board with green butcher paper.

2. Cut the snail shell from brown tagboard. Add a spiral line with a marking pen as shown. Glue the star (page 247) to the shell.

3. Cut the head and tail from yellow construction paper as shown. Add details to the head with a black marking pen. Tape pieces of pipe cleaner to the snail's head for tentacles.

4. Pin the snail to the bulletin board. Then pin a long strip of plastic wrap loosely behind the snail to form its shiny trail.

5. Pin the caption to the board. Pin student work along the shiny trail.

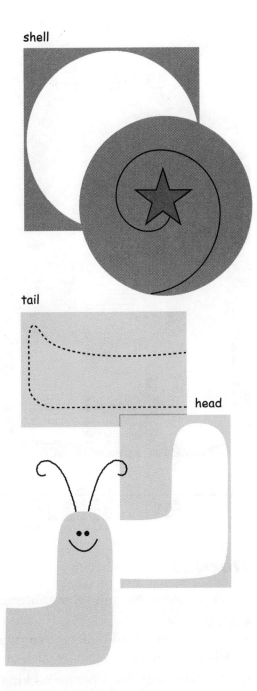

shell

tail

head

Other Ways to Use This Board

Remove "of Shining Work." Use the board to display facts about snails. Mount pictures on construction paper. Write facts on cards. Post these on the snail's trail. Students use the information posted to write reports or descriptive paragraphs.

Snails have hard shells.

Snails leave a sticky trail.

Snails have two sets of tentacles.

Snails eat plants.

Reaching for Good Work

Materials

- background—blue and yellow butcher paper
- octopus:
  body and tentacles—pink butcher paper
  suckers—bottle caps or shiny stick-on dots
- yellow construction paper for backing student work
- cutouts:
  caption on pages 249, 251, and 253, laminated and trimmed
  eyes on page 253, laminated and trimmed

Put It Together

1. Cover the bulletin board with blue paper. Add a wavy strip of yellow to the top of the bulletin board.

2. Cut the octopus from pink butcher paper as shown.

3. Add the eyes (page 253) to the octopus. Draw on a mouth with a black marking pen. Pin the body to the bulletin board.

4. Glue bottle caps or stick-on dots on the tentacles for suckers. Add the tentacles to the octopus. Pin them so they twist and turn.

5. Pin the caption within the yellow border.

6. Pin student work to the board.

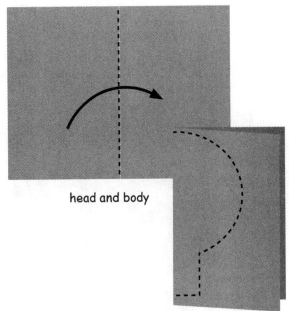

head and body

8 tentacles

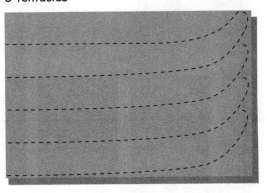

Other Ways to Use This Board

Write "Books" on a piece of tagboard. Use it to replace "Work" in the caption. Pin a book jacket on each tentacle to encourage students to read nonfiction books about creatures that live in the sea.

Hear Ye! Hear Ye!

Materials

- background—yellow butcher paper
- scroll—white butcher paper
- page—clothing may be any bright color you choose
  sleeve—9" x 9" (23 x 23 cm) square
  torso—9" x 12" (23 x 30.5 cm)
  leg and arm—9" x 12" (23 x 30.5 cm)
- trumpet—3" x 18" (7.5 x 45.5 cm) yellow construction paper
- assorted construction paper for mounting student work
- cutouts:
  caption on pages 255 and 257, laminated and trimmed
  page's head on page 259, laminated and trimmed
  boot on page 261, laminated and trimmed

Put It Together

1. Cover the bulletin board with yellow butcher paper.

2. Make a scroll by rolling white butcher paper at the top and bottom. Pin it to the board.

3. Cut out the page's head (page 259) and boot (page 261). Cut the remaining parts from construction paper as shown. Add details to the sleeve with a marking pen or scraps of paper.

4. Pin all parts of the page to the bulletin board.

5. Make a trumpet from yellow construction paper. Pin the trumpet to the board. Bend the page's arm around to hold the trumpet.

6. Pin the caption to the board.

7. Mount student work on colored construction paper and pin it to the scroll.

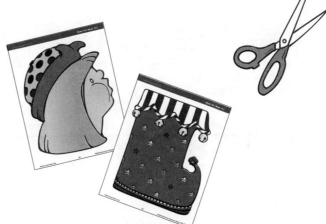

Other Ways to Use This Board

Use the scroll to post homework or long-term assignments. Post a sign saying "This work needs to be done." Write the tasks on colored sentence strips and post on the scroll. Change as necessary.

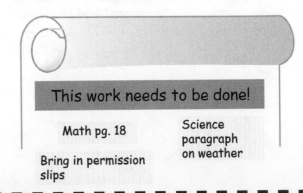

This work needs to be done!

Math pg. 18

Science paragraph on weather

Bring in permission slips

Sailing on a Sea of GOOD WORK

Materials

- background—yellow and blue butcher paper
- sailboats:
  four 9" x 12" (23 x 30.5 cm) pieces of assorted colored construction paper
  black construction paper scraps
- yellow construction paper for backing student work
- cutouts:
  sign on page 263, laminated and trimmed
  caption on page 265, laminated and trimmed
  sails on pages 267, 269, 271, and 273, laminated and trimmed

Put It Together

1. Cover the top third of the bulletin board with yellow paper. Pin blue butcher paper to the rest of the board, scalloped to look like ripples in the water.

2. Make the sailboats.

   Cut the bottom halves of the sailboats from the four colored pieces of construction paper. Attach the sails to the boats using a piece of black construction paper. Then cut out the letters W-O-R-K (page 265) and glue them to the colored boats in order.

3. Pin the sign (page 263) in the top left-hand corner of the board.

4. Add student work.

Other Ways to Use This Board

Brainstorm with students to create a list of ways to guarantee good work. List these on sentence strips. Post the strips on the bulletin board as a reminder.

concentrate   listen carefully   read directions   check your work

Whoooo did this good work?

Materials

- background—dark blue butcher paper
- tree trunk and branch—black butcher paper
- moon—white butcher paper
- yellow construction paper for mounting student work
- cutouts:
  caption on pages 275, 277, and 279, laminated and trimmed
  owl on page 281, laminated and trimmed

Put It Together

1. Cover the bulletin board with dark blue paper. Cut a moon from the white paper as shown. Pin the moon in one corner of the board.

2. Make the tree from black butcher paper. Twist the paper to form the trunk and branch. Pin these securely to the bulletin board.

3. Pin the owl (page 281) on the tree branch.

4. Pin the caption across the top of the board.

5. Mount student work on yellow construction paper and pin it to the board.

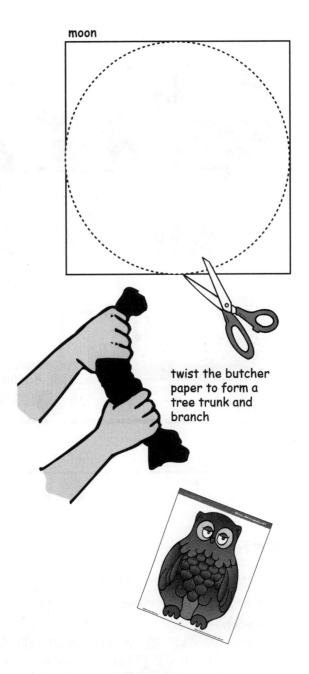

moon

twist the butcher paper to form a tree trunk and branch

Other Ways to Use This Board

Remove "did this good work." Leave "Whoooo…?" Have students write a riddle. Post these on the bulletin board and challenge the rest of the class to try to determine from the information in the riddle, who or what it is about.

Riddles might be about…

- classmates
- other nocturnal animals
- other birds

All Aboard!

Materials

Note: This board takes a large space, as you will be making a car for each student in your class.

- background—yellow butcher paper
- each train car:
  car—9" x 12" (23 x 30.5 cm) assorted colors of construction paper
  wheels—3" x 3" (7.5 cm) square of black construction paper for each wheel
  name tag—3" x 6" (7.5 x 15 cm) white construction paper
- smoke—cotton balls
- train track—black roving
- assorted construction paper for mounting student work
- cutouts:
  caption on pages 283 and 285, laminated and trimmed
  engine on pages 287 and 289, laminated and trimmed
  caboose on page 291, laminated and trimmed

Put It Together

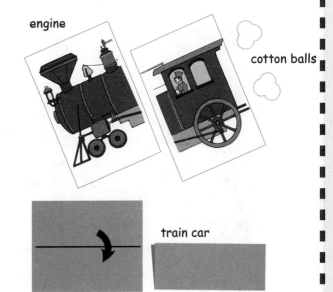

engine

cotton balls

1. Cover the bulletin board with yellow butcher paper.

2. Cut out the train engine (pages 287 and 289). Pin it to the board. Add cotton ball smoke puffs coming out of the smokestack. (Pull the cotton balls apart to make them larger.)

3. Pin the caption to the bulletin board.

4. Make a train car for each of your students. Fold the construction paper in half lengthwise, and staple at the ends. Cut round black wheels and glue them to the cars. Add a white strip of paper with each student's name to each car.

5. Staple the cars in a curving line after the engine. The caboose is at the end (page 291). Pin black roving below the cars for the train track.

6. Slip student work in the train car pockets.

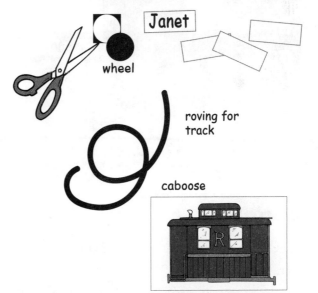

train car

Janet

wheel

roving for track

caboose

Other Ways to Use This Board

Use the train to create a year-long class time line. Make a car for each month of the year. Slip samples of special activities for each month in its train car. During the last week of school, go through each car to review what happened that month.

September

October

November

Braggin' Dragon

Materials

- background—blue butcher paper
- dragon:
  body and arms—green corrugated or butcher paper
  ears and eyelids—green corrugated or butcher paper scraps
  nostrils—red construction paper scraps
  horns—yellow construction paper scraps
  eyes—white construction paper scraps
- fire—orange tissue paper
- construction paper for mounting student work
- cutouts—caption on pages 293, 295, and 297, laminated and trimmed

Put It Together

1. Cover the top third of the bulletin board with blue butcher paper.

2. Cut the dragon's body from green paper as shown. Pin it on the bulletin board. Cut out the ears, arms, and tail and pin them in place.

3. Make the dragon's face.

   Cut two spirals from red construction paper for nostrils.

   Cut the eyes from white construction paper. Cut the eyelids from green butcher paper scraps as shown. Add details with a black marking pen.

   Cut the horns from yellow construction paper.

4. Pin the pieces to the dragon's head.

5. Crumple orange tissue paper and pin it to the nostrils to represent fire.

6. Pin the caption in place. Pin student work to the dragon's body.

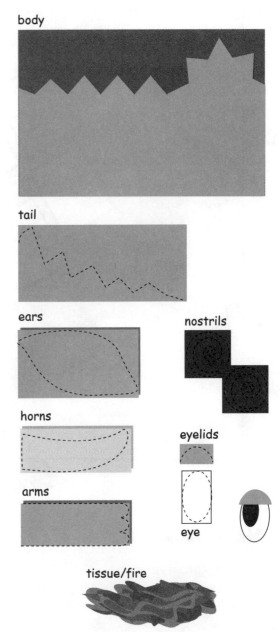

body

tail

ears

nostrils

horns

eyelids

arms

eye

tissue/fire

Other Ways to Use This Board

Use the board to display literature about dragons. Post dragon poems written on tagboard. Post the book covers or cards containing titles of dragon stories. (Have all of the books referenced available in class for students to use.)

Once Upon A Time
Dragons flew over castles,
Dragons flew up in the clouds.
Flocks of dragons filled the sky,
Flying in graceful crowds.

Super Kids

Materials

- background:
  sky—blue butcher paper
  clouds—white butcher paper

- Super Kid:
  cape—yellow butcher paper or cloth
  gloves—9" x 12" (23 x 30.5 cm) red construction paper
  boots—12" x 18" (30.5 x 45.5 cm) brown construction paper

- dark blue construction paper for mounting student work

- cutouts:
  caption on page 299, laminated and trimmed
  face on page 301, laminated and trimmed
  S on page 303, laminated and trimmed

Put It Together

1. Cover the bulletin board with blue butcher paper. Cut clouds from white butcher paper and pin them to the board.

2. Cut Super Kid's cape from yellow butcher paper or cloth. Pin the cape to the board.

3. Make the Super Kid.

   Trace a student's hands on red construction paper to create gloves.

   Cut the boots from the brown construction paper.

   Pin the gloves, boots, and face (page 301) to the cape.

4. Cut out the large *S* (page 303) and glue it to the center of the cape.

5. Add the caption to the bulletin board. Then pin student work on the cape.

cloud

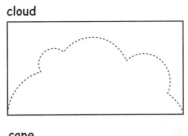

cape

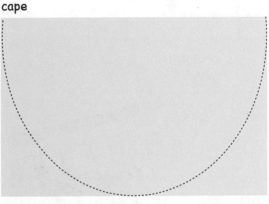

gloves   boots

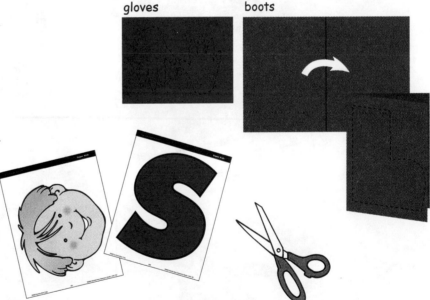

Other Ways to Use This Board

Have students write descriptive paragraphs about themselves, describing a way in which they are "Super Kids." Pin the paragraphs to the bulletin board. Pin a photograph of each child with his or her paragraph.

 Bulletin Boards Every Classroom Needs • EMC 787

Bulletin Board Cutouts

This book provides full-color cutouts to make creating bulletin boards easier for you. All cutouts should be

- removed from the book,
- laminated, and
- trimmed

Store your cutouts in an envelope paper-clipped to the direction pages. Since the letters and pictures are laminated, they can be used again and again.

Bulletin Boards Every Classroom Needs • EMC 787

Bulletin Boards Every Classroom Needs • EMC 787

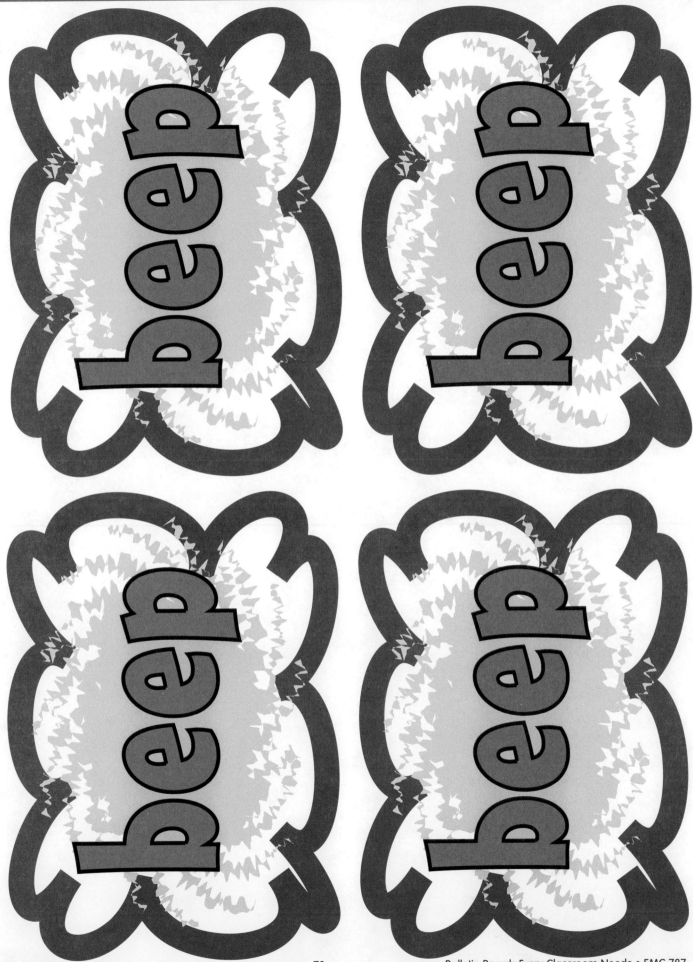

Bulletin Boards Every Classroom Needs • EMC 787

Bulletin Boards Every Classroom Needs • EMC 787

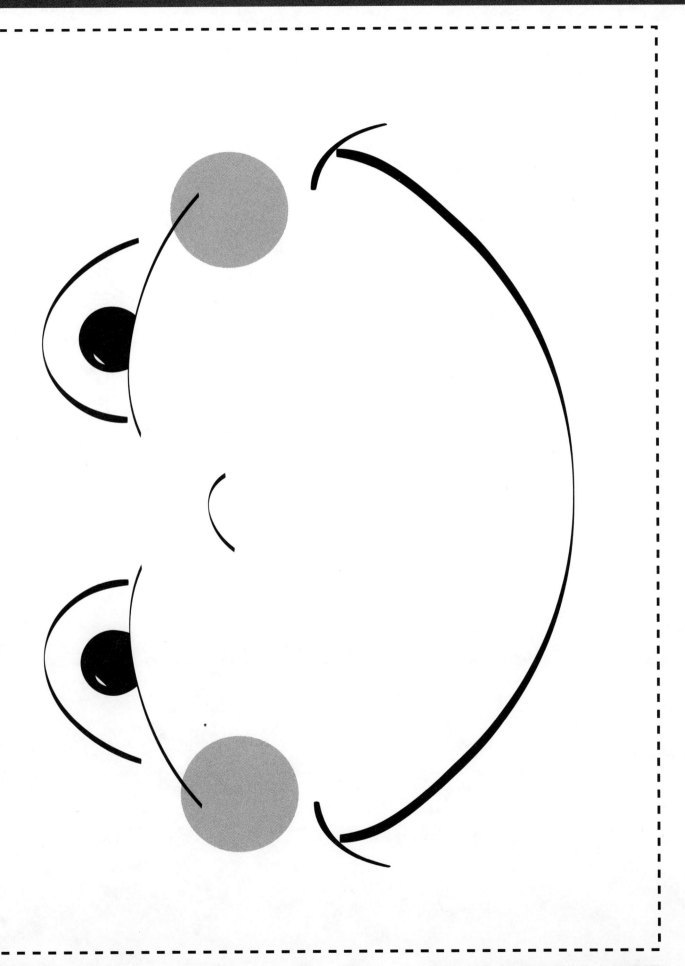

Bulletin Boards Every Classroom Needs • EMC 787

Bulletin Boards Every Classroom Needs • EMC 787

Bulletin Boards Every Classroom Needs • EMC 787

Bulletin Boards Every Classroom Needs • EMC 787

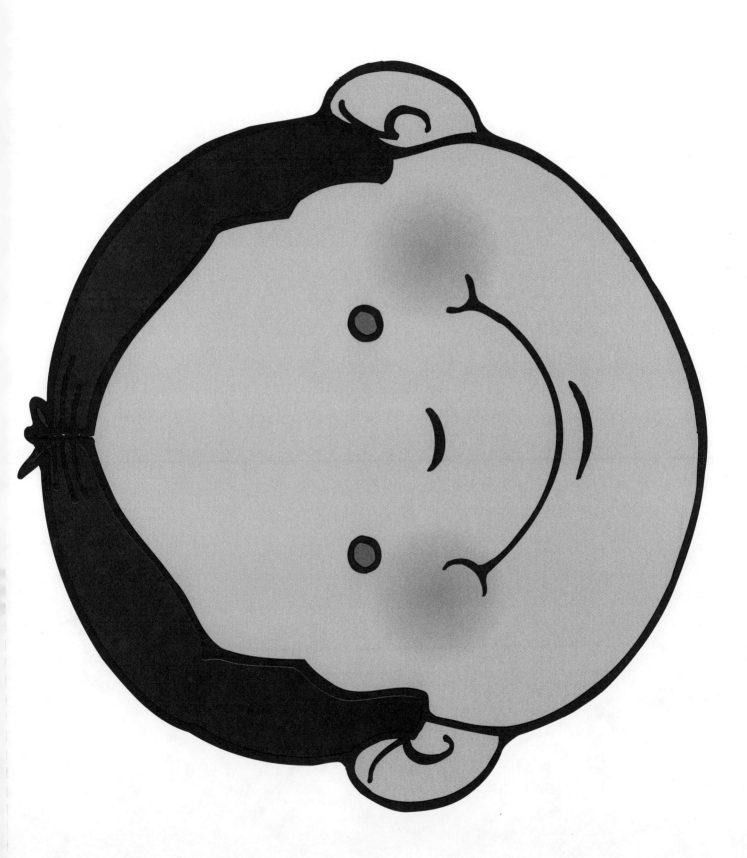

Bulletin Boards Every Classroom Needs • EMC 787

Bulletin Boards Every Classroom Needs • EMC 787

Bulletin Boards Every Classroom Needs • EMC 787

8, 6, 4, 2,

What do we

appreciate?

Bulletin Boards Every Classroom Needs • EMC 787

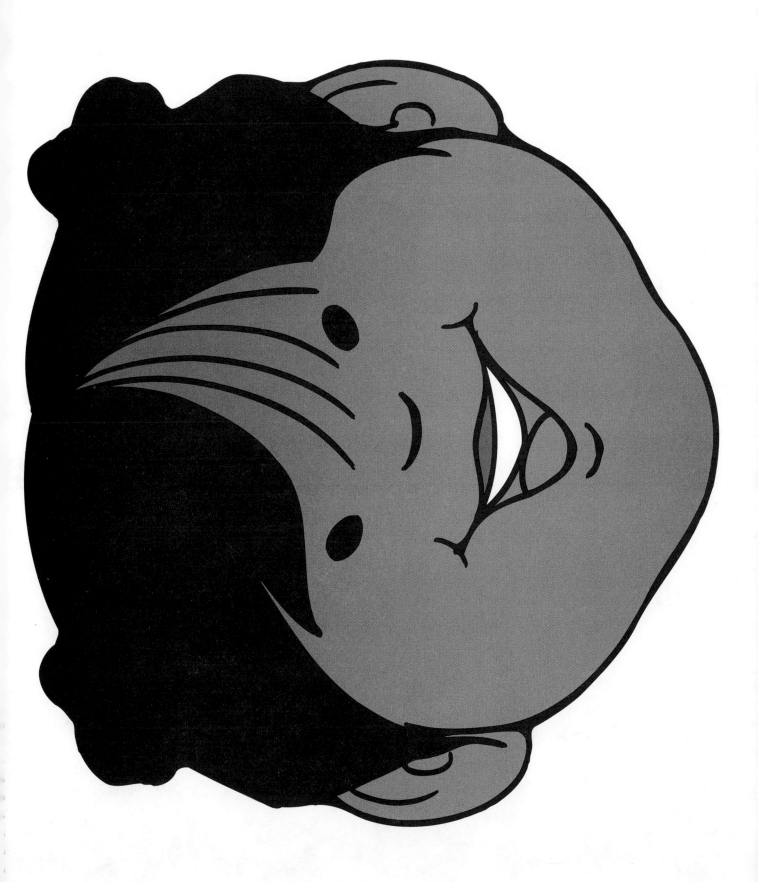

97

Bulletin Boards Every Classroom Needs • EMC 787

99

Bulletin Boards Every Classroom Needs • EMC 787

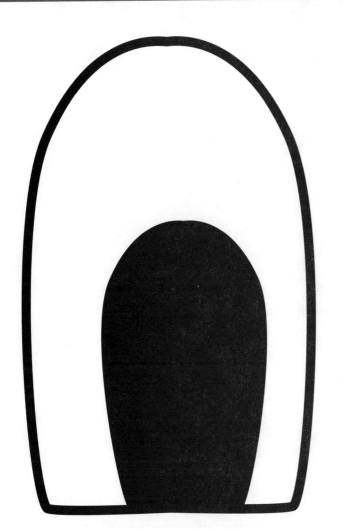
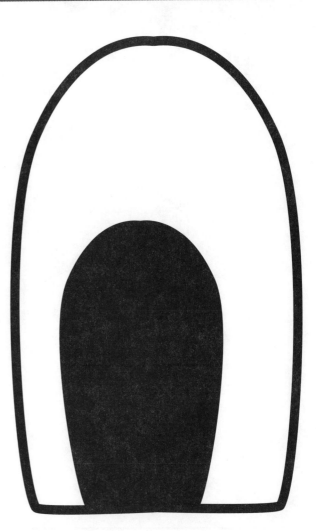

Bulletin Boards Every Classroom Needs • EMC 787

Bulletin Boards Every Classroom Needs • EMC 787

Bulletin Boards Every Classroom Needs • EMC 787

Bulletin Boards Every Classroom Needs • EMC 787

Bulletin Boards Every Classroom Needs • EMC 787

Bulletin Boards Every Classroom Needs • EMC 787

Bulletin Boards Every Classroom Needs • EMC 787

Bulletin Boards Every Classroom Needs • EMC 787

Bulletin Boards Every Classroom Needs • EMC 787

Bulletin Boards Every Classroom Needs • EMC 787

Bulletin Boards Every Classroom Needs • EMC 787

Bulletin Boards Every Classroom Needs • EMC 787

Bulletin Boards Every Classroom Needs • EMC 787

Bulletin Boards Every Classroom Needs • EMC 787

Bulletin Boards Every Classroom Needs • EMC 787

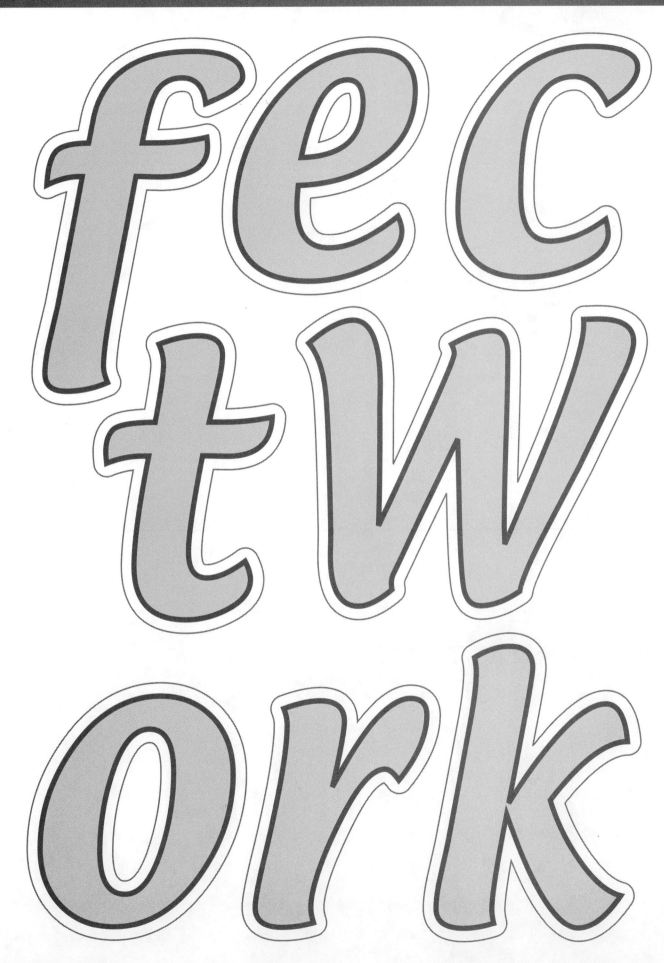

Bulletin Boards Every Classroom Needs • EMC 787

Bulletin Boards Every Classroom Needs • EMC 787

Bulletin Boards Every Classroom Needs • EMC 787

Bulletin Boards Every Classroom Needs • EMC 787

Bulletin Boards Every Classroom Needs • EMC 787

Bulletin Boards Every Classroom Needs • EMC 787

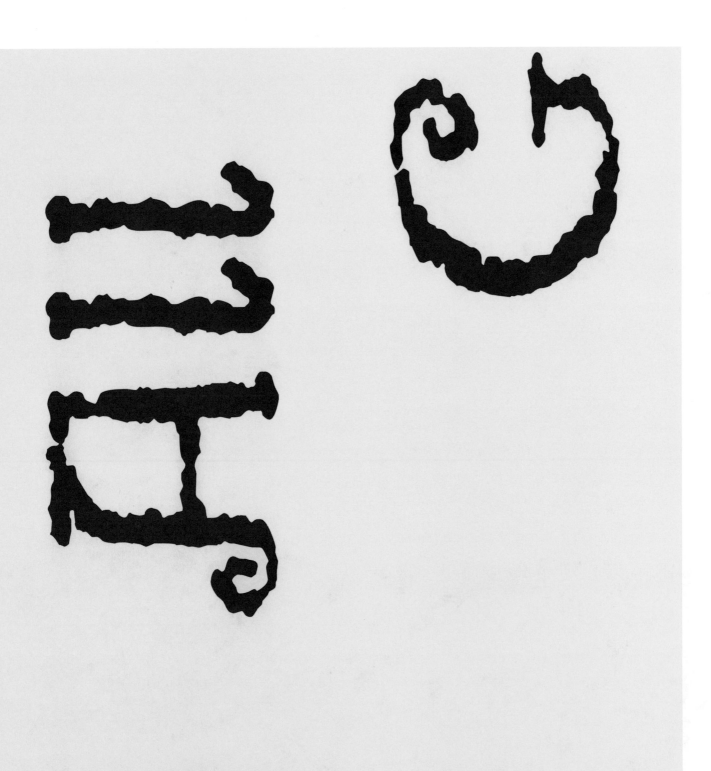

Bulletin Boards Every Classroom Needs • EMC 787

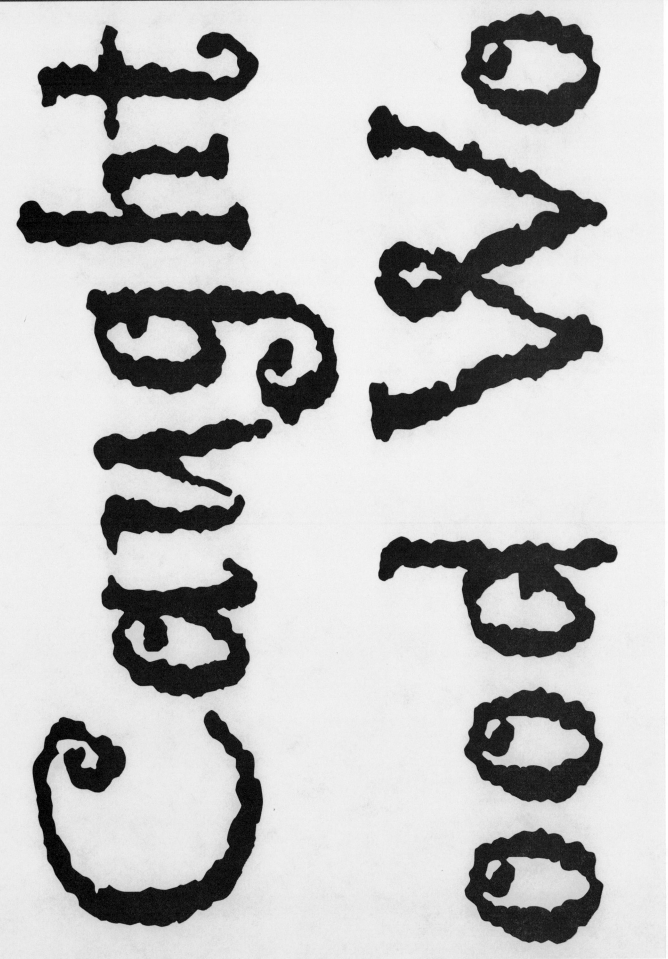

Bulletin Boards Every Classroom Needs • EMC 787

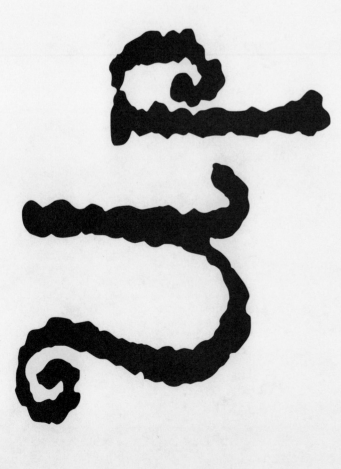

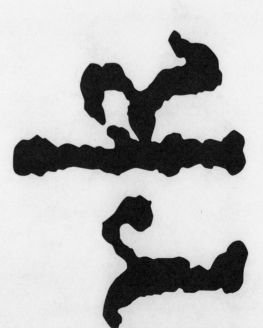

Bulletin Boards Every Classroom Needs • EMC 787

Bulletin Boards Every Classroom Needs • EMC 787

Bulletin Boards Every Classroom Needs • EMC 787

Bulletin Boards Every Classroom Needs • EMC 787

Bulletin Boards Every Classroom Needs • EMC 787

Bulletin Boards Every Classroom Needs • EMC 787

Bulletin Boards Every Classroom Needs • EMC 787

Bulletin Boards Every Classroom Needs • EMC 787

Bulletin Boards Every Classroom Needs • EMC 787

Bulletin Boards Every Classroom Needs • EMC 787

Bulletin Boards Every Classroom Needs • EMC 787

Bulletin Boards Every Classroom Needs • EMC 787

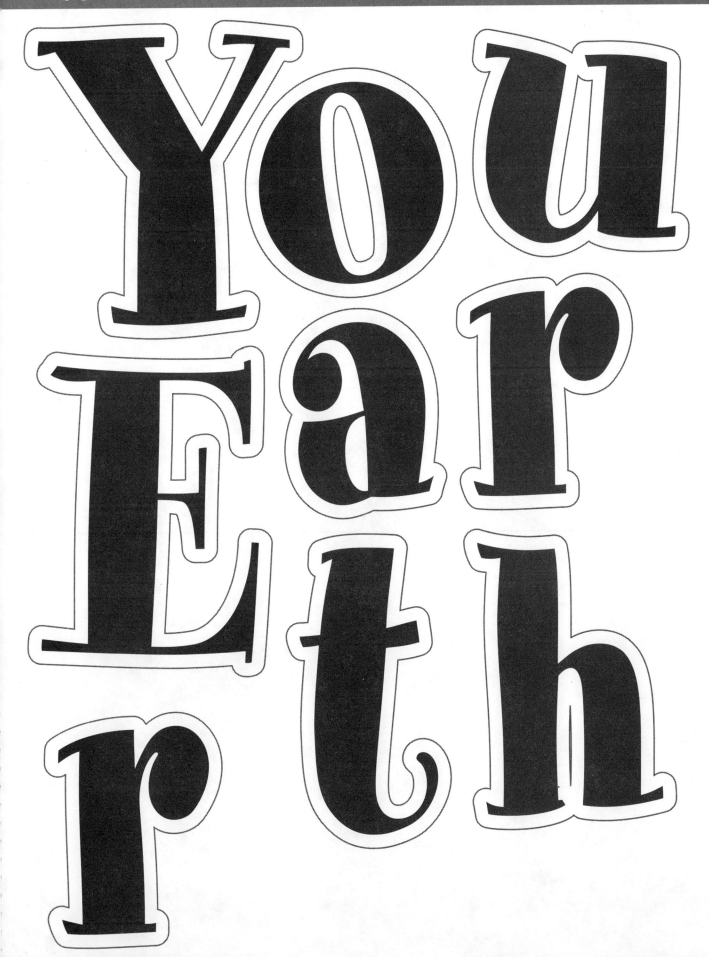

Bulletin Boards Every Classroom Needs • EMC 787

194

Thi
sow
kro

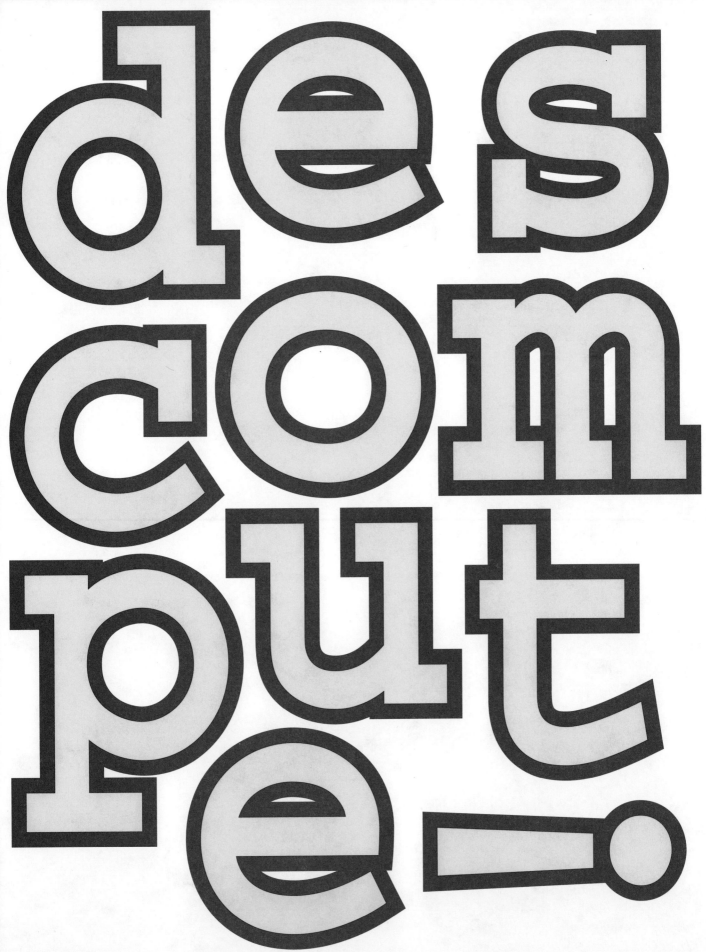

Bulletin Boards Every Classroom Needs • EMC 787

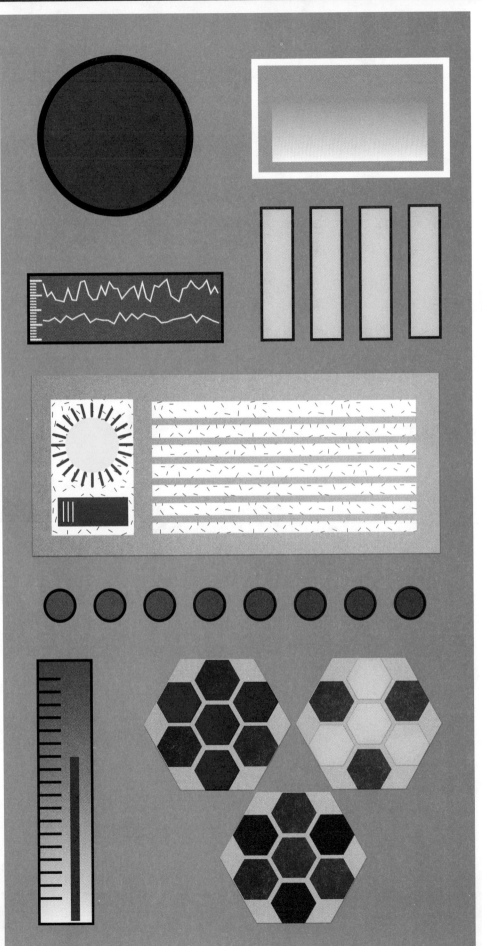

Bulletin Boards Every Classroom Needs • EMC 787

Bulletin Boards Every Classroom Needs • EMC 787

Bulletin Boards Every Classroom Needs • EMC 787

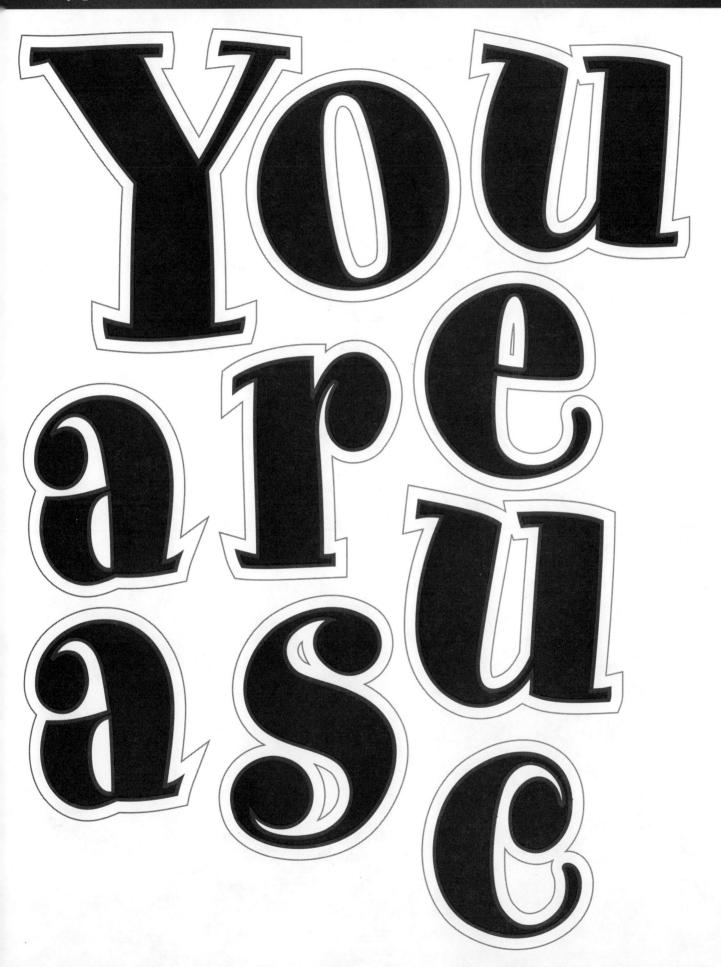

Bulletin Boards Every Classroom Needs • EMC 787

Bulletin Boards Every Classroom Needs • EMC 787

Bulletin Boards Every Classroom Needs • EMC 787

Good Work

Bulletin Boards Every Classroom Needs • EMC 787

Bulletin Boards Every Classroom Needs • EMC 787

Bulletin Boards Every Classroom Needs • EMC 787

Bulletin Boards Every Classroom Needs • EMC 787

Bulletin Boards Every Classroom Needs • EMC 787

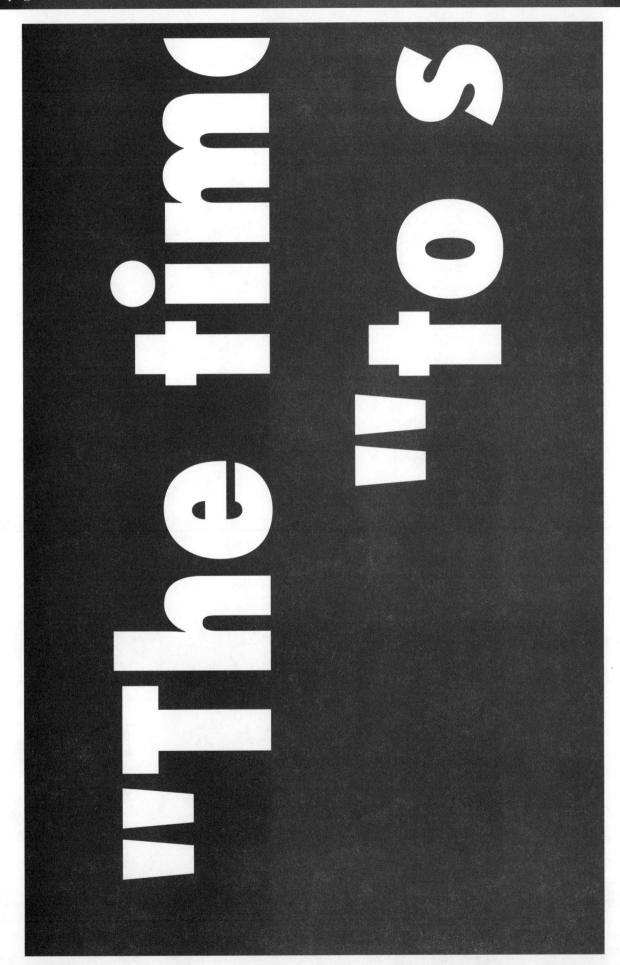

Bulletin Boards Every Classroom Needs • EMC 787

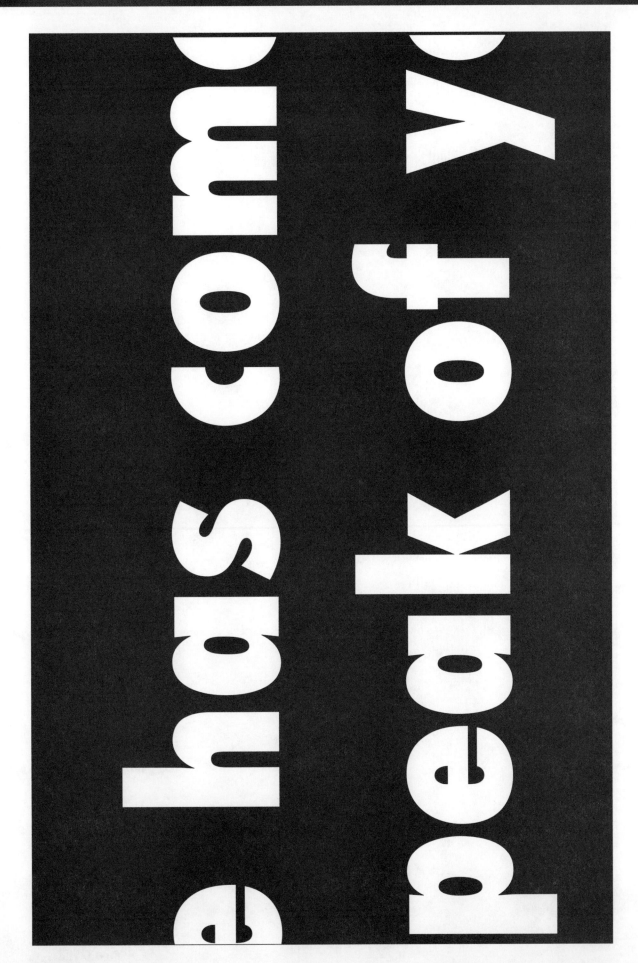

Bulletin Boards Every Classroom Needs • EMC 787

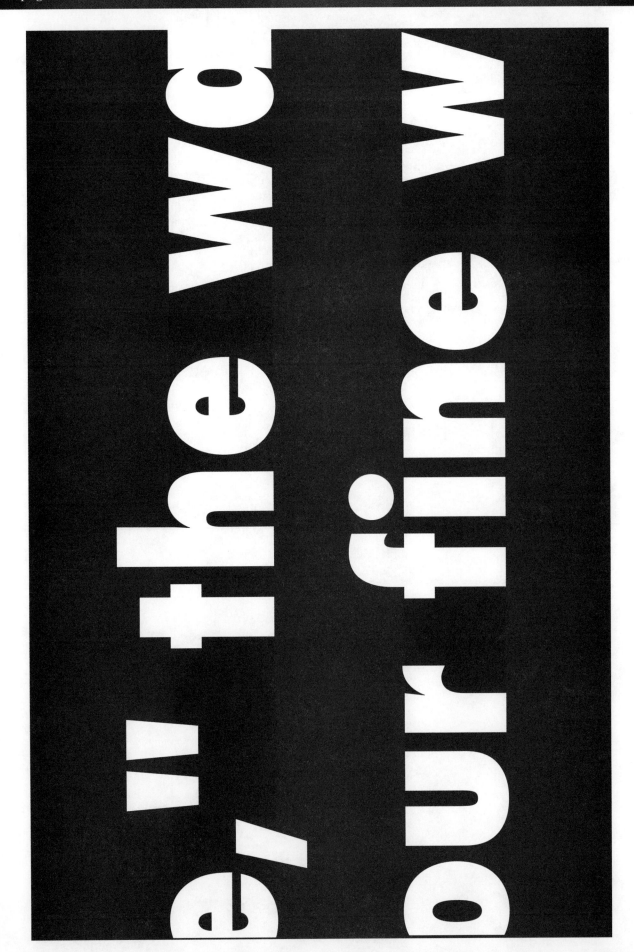

Bulletin Boards Every Classroom Needs • EMC 787

Bulletin Boards Every Classroom Needs • EMC 787

Bulletin Boards Every Classroom Needs • EMC 787

Bulletin Boards Every Classroom Needs • EMC 787

Bulletin Boards Every Classroom Needs • EMC 787

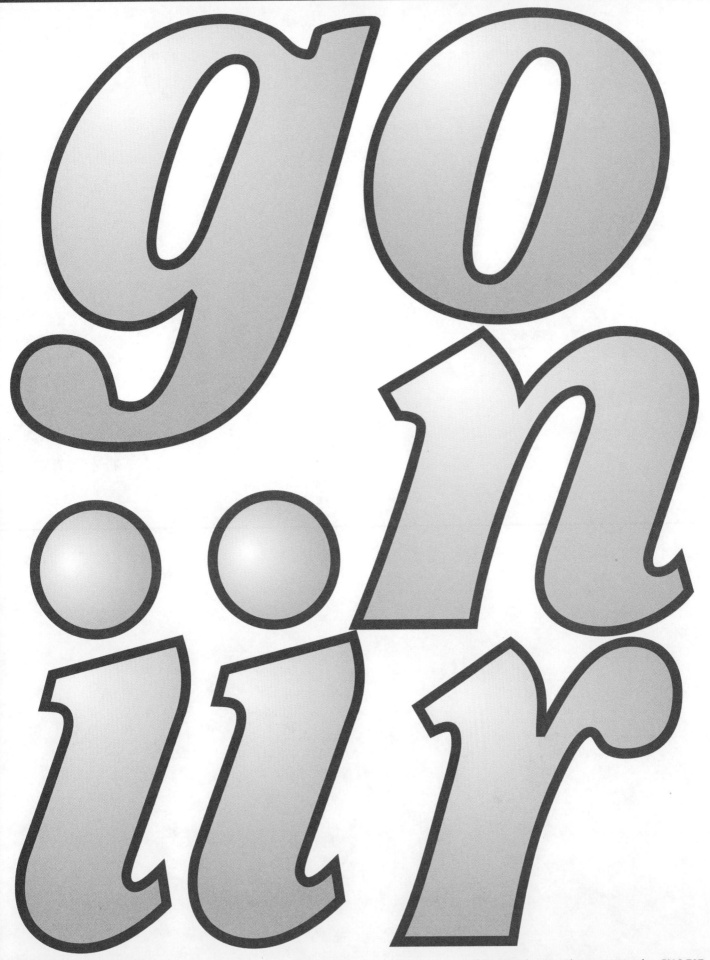

Bulletin Boards Every Classroom Needs • EMC 787

252

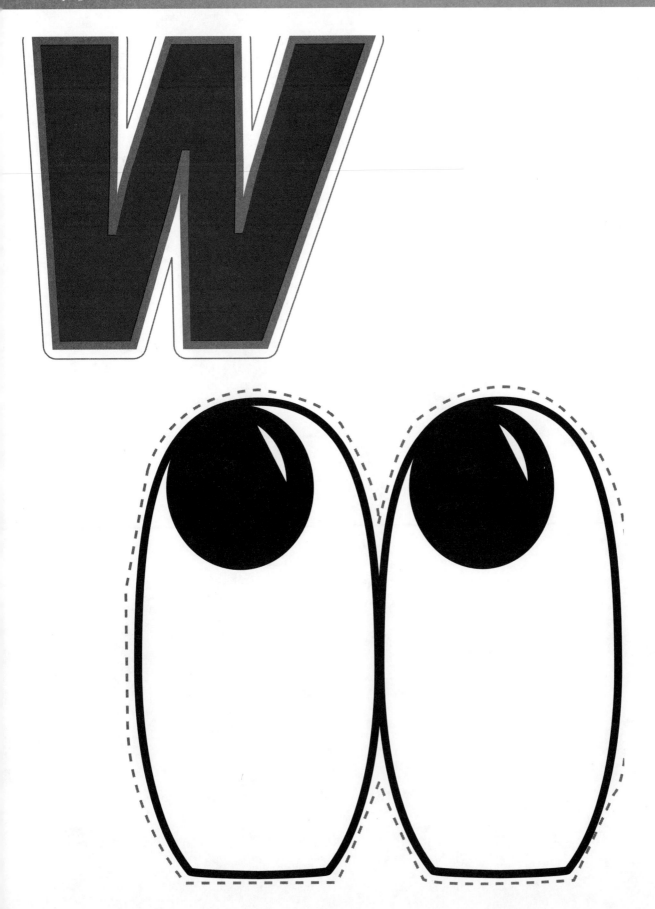

Bulletin Boards Every Classroom Needs • EMC 787

Bulletin Boards Every Classroom Needs • EMC 787

Bulletin Boards Every Classroom Needs • EMC 787

Bulletin Boards Every Classroom Needs • EMC 787

Bulletin Boards Every Classroom Needs • EMC 787

Bulletin Boards Every Classroom Needs • EMC 787

Bulletin Boards Every Classroom Needs • EMC 787

Bulletin Boards Every Classroom Needs • EMC 787

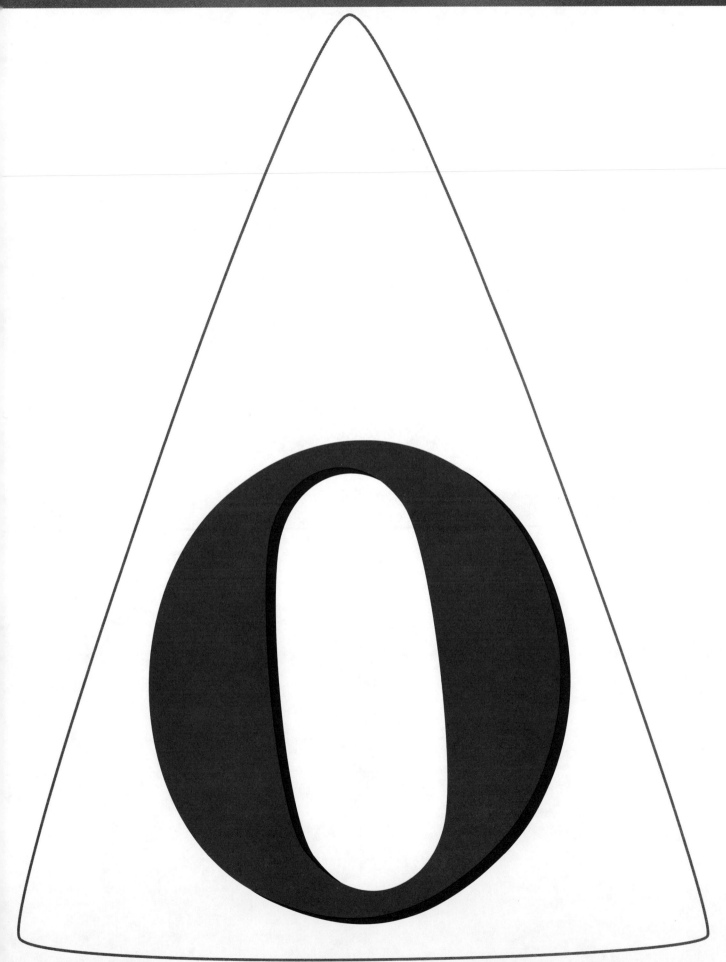

Bulletin Boards Every Classroom Needs • EMC 787

Bulletin Boards Every Classroom Needs • EMC 787

Bulletin Boards Every Classroom Needs • EMC 787

Bulletin Boards Every Classroom Needs • EMC 787

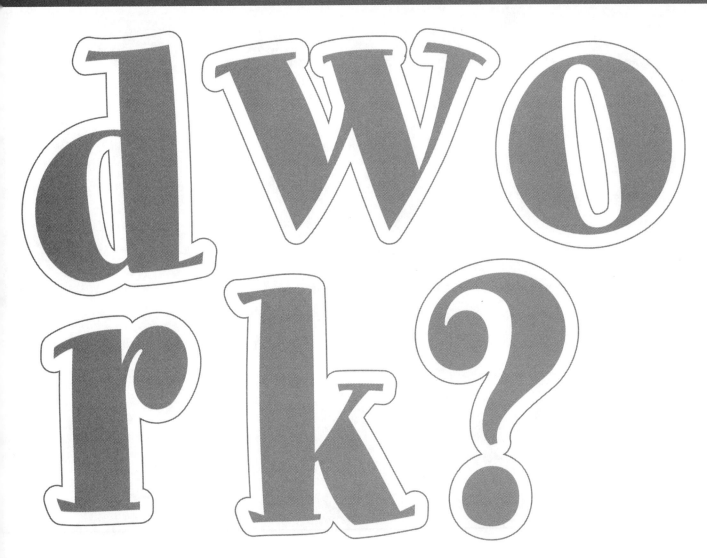

Bulletin Boards Every Classroom Needs • EMC 787

Bulletin Boards Every Classroom Needs • EMC 787

Bulletin Boards Every Classroom Needs • EMC 787

Bulletin Boards Every Classroom Needs • EMC 787

Bulletin Boards Every Classroom Needs • EMC 787

©2001 by Evan-Moor Corp.

288

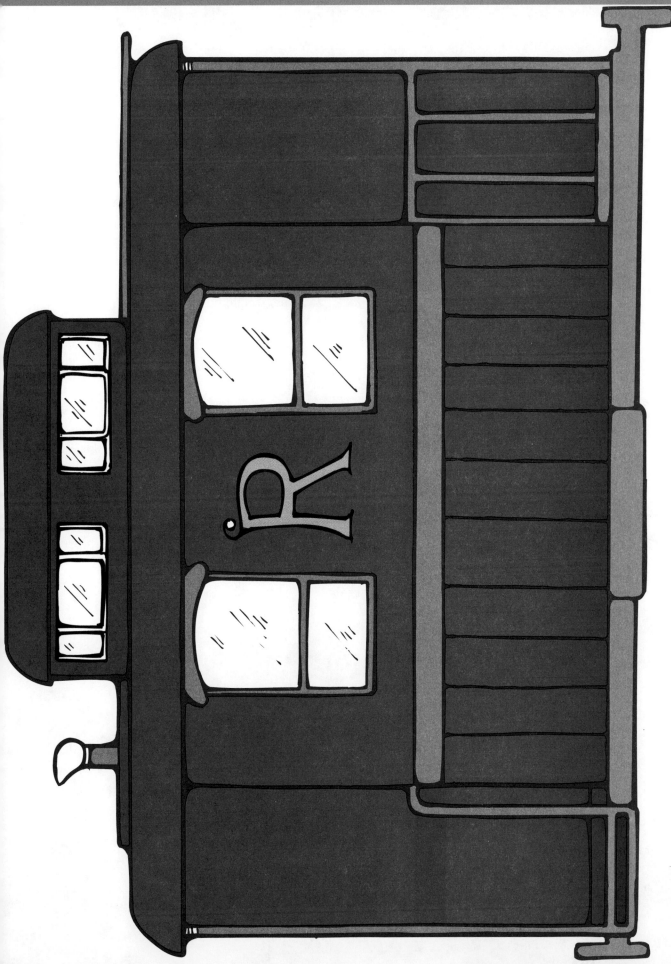

Bulletin Boards Every Classroom Needs • EMC 787

Bulletin Boards Every Classroom Needs • EMC 787

Bulletin Boards Every Classroom Needs • EMC 787

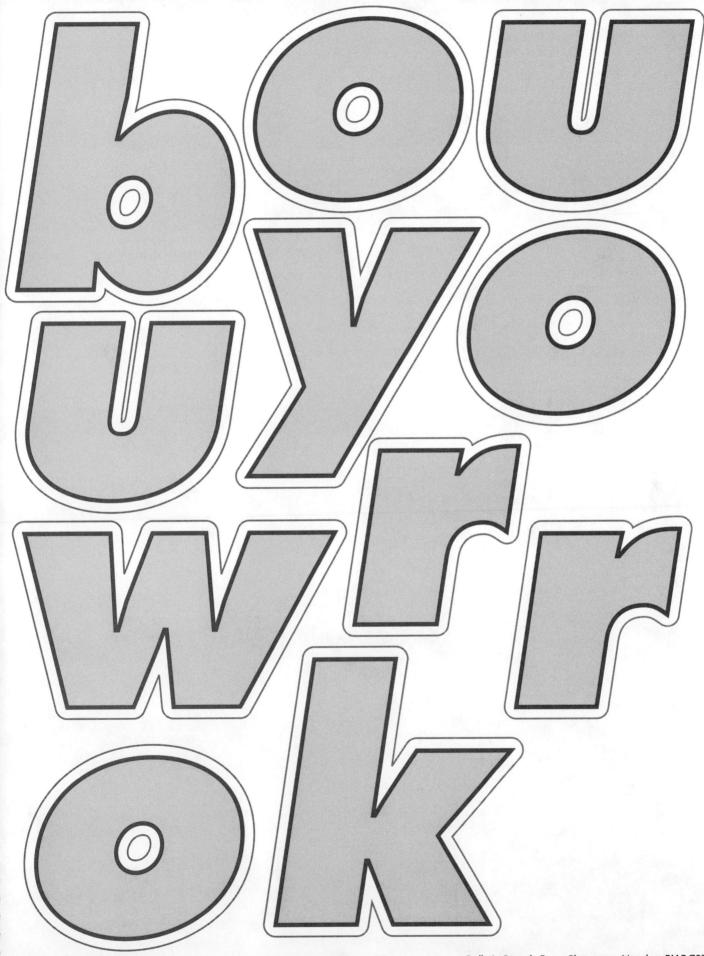

Bulletin Boards Every Classroom Needs • EMC 787

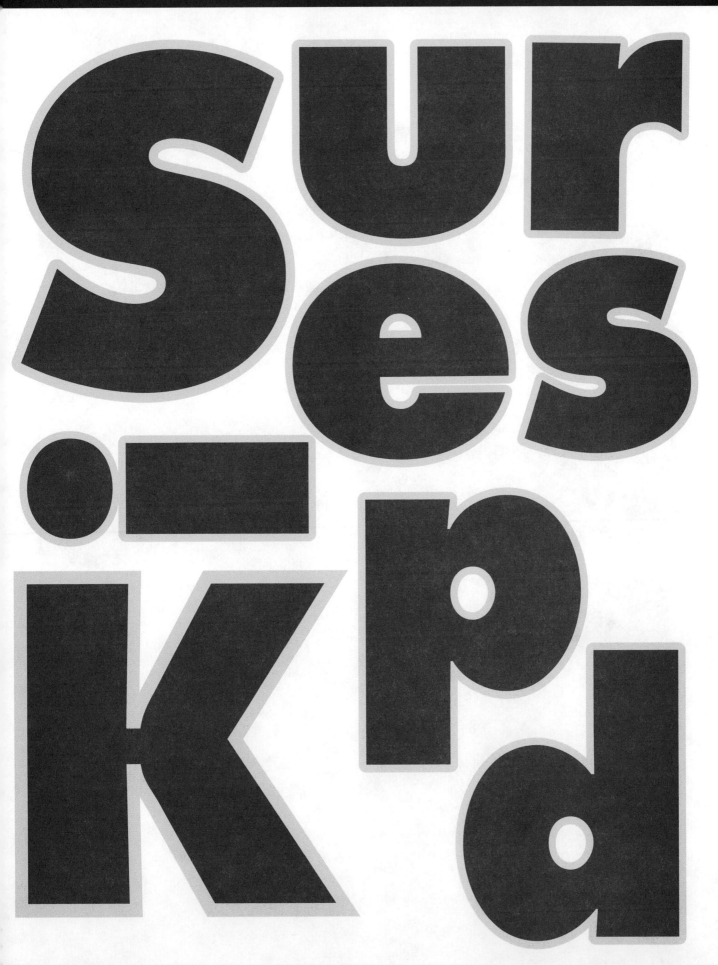

Bulletin Boards Every Classroom Needs • EMC 787

Bulletin Boards Every Classroom Needs • EMC 787